She is Free Indeed

A DEVOTIONAL

*FINDING STRENGTH AND HEALING IN JESUS
AFTER AN ABUSIVE RELATIONSHIP*

RACHEL COX

2nd PRINT EDITION
SHE IS FREE INDEED
Copyright © 2020 RACHEL COX
All rights reserved.

Bible translations used in this book:
The New Jerusalem Bible (NJB) The Passion Translation (TPT)
The New International Version (NIV) The Amplified Bible (AMP)
The English Standard Version (ESV) The New American Standard Bible (NASB)
The New King James Bible (NKJ) The Good News Translation (GNT)
The New Living Translation (NLT) The King James Bible (KJV)
The Complete Jewish Bible (CJB) God's Word Translation (GWT)
The Message (MSG)

Characteristics of certain translations including italicized words and the use of "LORD" have been retained in this book. Hebrew references from Strong's Concordance and Strong's Exhaustive Concordance unless otherwise noted.

LIBRARY AND ARCHIVES CANADA DATA
ISBN: 978-1-989456-361

Without limiting the rights under copyright reserved above, no part of this publication may be reproduced, stored in or introduced into a retrieval system, or transmitted, in any form or by any means (electronic, mechanical, photocopying, recording or otherwise), without the prior written permission of both the copyright owner and the above publisher of this book.

The scanning, uploading, and distribution of this book via the Internet or via any other means without permission of the publisher is illegal and punishable by law. Please purchase only authorized electronic editions and do not participate in or encourage electronic piracy of copyright materials. Your support of the author's rights is appreciated.

So if the Son sets you free, you will be free indeed.
John 8:36 (NIV)

He heals the broken-hearted and binds up their wounds. Psalm 147:3 (NIV)

"There are times you must risk unraveling the life you have in order to create the life God wants for you."
Leslie Vernick, The Emotionally Destructive Marriage: How to Find Your Voice and Reclaim Your Hope

Dedication

To Elsie Goerzen, a giver of light

Introduction

The end of an abusive relationship is an extraordinarily difficult season. It is like an emotional volcano. You are likely experiencing a great variety of feelings, both positive and negative. There have been years of pain and damage to your body and soul, and while leaving is the right thing to do, it doesn't make all of the pain go away. There will be moments where you feel joyful and elated, and others where you feel utter despair. At times you might feel exhilaratingly free and others like you have lost your right arm. Fear may be your predominant emotion. This is all very normal.

If you allow Him in, this is the time in your life where you will feel the Lord's presence most keenly. He will step in and husband you. Isaiah 54:5 (NIV) reads, "For your Maker is your husband-- the LORD Almighty is his name-- the Holy One of Israel is your Redeemer; he is called the God of all the earth." He will be there for you every moment, collecting your tears and feeling your pain. There are no 10 steps for guaranteed healing, nor does it come quickly. But as you wait upon and enter into intimacy with the Lord, He will meet you and He will heal your soul.

My hope is that as you read these devotionals that they would help you on your journey to healing as they point you to Jesus, our Healer.

1

"Come now and let's deliberate over the next steps to take together. Yahweh promises you over and over "Though your sins stain you like scarlet, I will whiten them like bright, new-fallen snow! Even though they are deep red like crimson, they will be made white like wool!" If you have a willing heart to let me help you, and if you will obey me, you will feast on the blessings of abundant harvest."
Isaiah 1:18-19 (TPT)

The most important thing we need to know is that Jesus has covered our sin. When we bring our pain and burdens to Him, to the cross, He performs an exchange.

He gives peace for fear.
He gives hope for disappointment.
He gives joy for sorrow.
He gives light for darkness.
He gives strength for weakness.
He gives love for hate.
He gives faith for anxiety.

No one is perfect and no one escapes a relationship without some guilt. But the first thing Jesus wants to do is to wipe away our guilt and shame. They are not for us to bear. He wants to free you from that bondage so that you can walk forward with him in perfect trust that he is going to heal your wounds. So, come before the cross today and one by one lay all of those things down and listen to Him as He shows you

She is Free Indeed

---

what He is giving you in return. Accept the freedom that Jesus gives you

Now the enemy will attack you. He is going to try to put that guilt and shame back on you and he will use your former partner against you. Expect it. But know that every single day you can come back before the cross and release those things over and over and over again. Your Father has forgiven you and He has set you free. Hold tightly to those truths.

"Yes, Zion will be redeemed with justice and her repentant converts with righteousness." Isaiah 1:27 (TPT)

Reflection: What would you like to exchange with the Lord today? Make a list and then let Him give you good things in return.

Prayer: *Jesus, show me what I need to lay down today. Help me to accept the truth that You take on all of those things, and that I don't need to carry them anymore. I lay before You my ... (guilt, shame, hurt, anger, etc.). thank You for healing me and setting me free.*

2

"It will happen in the final days that the mountain of Yahweh's house will rise higher than the mountains and tower above the heights. Then all the nations will stream to it, many peoples will come to it and say, 'Come, let us go up to the mountain of Yahweh, to the house of the God of Jacob that he may teach us his ways so that we may walk in his paths.' For the Law will issue from Zion and the word of Yahweh from Jerusalem." Isaiah 2:2-3 (NJB)

Abusive relationships strongly affect our minds. You have been lied to, lied about and have been told many things that have confused you. You may have difficulty relating to God as your Father because of the things your partner may have said about Him. Spiritual abuse is very often found in relationships where the abusive partner claims to be a Christian. There are many different types of abuse and the further you come out of the relationship you will recognize more and more things that your partner did to you that were abusive.

The first thing you need to take back is your mind. You need to turn your eyes toward the heights, you need to ask the Lord to rid your mind of the lies that were planted there throughout your relationship, and to teach you His ways so that you may walk in His paths. You need to give the Lord control of the areas that your partner tried to dominate you. Immerse yourself in the Word and in worship. There is so much healing that comes simply through entering

She is Free Indeed

God's Presence in worship. Like everything, this is a process. Take the first step today.

*"The arrogant will be humbled
and the pride of man brought low.
Only one will be exalted in that day: Yahweh!" Isaiah 2:11
(TPT)*

Reflection: Take some time today to spend in God's word and ask Him what truths He wants you to hear from Him today.

Prayer: *Jesus take my former partner's voice out of my head. I want You to take that place, I want your authority to reign over my life. Guard my mind against the lies of the enemy. Help me to know only Your truth.*

3

"Then Yahweh will create over all of Mount Zion and over every gathering a cloud of smoke by day and a glow of flaming fire by night. And all this manifestation of dazzling glory will spread over them like a wedding canopy. It will be a tabernacle as a shade from the scorching heat of the day and a safe shelter to protect them from the storm and rain." Isaiah 4:5-6 (TPT)

Note the word, "canopy," in the verses above. While most translations use the word, "canopy," or "tent," the original word in Hebrew is, *chaphaph*, which means, to enclose, surround and cover. It is related to the word, *chuppa*, which is the canopy under which a Jewish couple is married.

What does it mean for the Lord to be your husband? While that word may be difficult to think about given what you have experienced, it means that He wants to *enclose* you in His loving arms. It means that he wants to *surround* you with songs of deliverance. It means that he wants to *cover* you with His protection. But the Lord does not ever force anything on us. He offers himself, and waits for us to accept. His arms are open wide, waiting for you, longing for you to come running into them. He wants to heal your wounded heart; he wants to wipe your tears away. He wants to be everything to you that your former partner was not. Jesus laid His life down for you because He loved you so much. It is going to take time and healing before you are able to engage with the notion of a husband being a positive thing, but you can still embrace what the Lord is offering you now.

Take another step towards Him today and let Him show you how He wants to meet your needs and show His mercy and grace. He will never abuse you in any way.

*"But he was pierced for our transgressions,
he was crushed for our iniquities;
the punishment that brought us peace was on him,
and by his wounds we are healed." Isaiah 53:5 (NIV)*

Reflection: What does the word, "husband," mean to you? Are you willing to let the Lord change that definition?

Prayer: Jesus, thank You for your incredible love. Thank You for the healing and strength you are going to give me. I come before You and ask You to enclose, surround and cover me, this day and every day.

4

"Then one of the seraphs flew to me, holding in its hand a live coal which it had taken from the altar with a pair of tongs. With this it touched my mouth and said: 'Look, this has touched your lips, your guilt has been removed and your sin forgiven.'" "I then heard the voice of the Lord saying: 'Whom shall I send? Who will go for us?' And I said, 'Here am I, send me.' He said: 'Go, and say to this people, "Listen and listen, but never understand! Look and look, but never perceive!"' Isaiah 6:6-9 (NJB)

Leslie Vernick, the author of, *The Emotionally Destructive Relationship*, writes, "God cares about your safety. He does not value the sanctity of marriage more than your safety and sanity.."[1] You may have friends and family who don't understand your to leave. Your church may not stand by you. Your children might be in distress. You yourself may be questioning your own decision.

You are probably dealing with a certain degree of guilt. It is difficult to untangle the web of an abusive relationship. It may have taken you a very long time to realize that you were, in fact, being abused. Abusers are masters of manipulation. They mess with your head. They make you believe that you are the crazy one.

Come before the Lord's altar. He led you out of bondage and He wants to take your guilt away. You need to know that the mistakes you made have been

---

1. https://leslievernick.com/if-i-leave-it-will-only-get-worse/

She is Free Indeed

forgiven. And now God has a plan for you! He has good plans for you! That might be hard to see now, and even months and years from now. But hold onto His promises. Brian Simmonds writes, "Your enemies will neither disturb you or distract you from My love, for under My wings you live and function and have your true identity."[2]

"Come now, let us settle the matter," says the LORD. "Though your sins are like scarlet, they shall be as white as snow; though they are red as crimson, they shall be like wool." Isaiah 1:18 (NIV)

Reflection: Do you believe that you stand before the Lord clothed in the righteousness of Jesus? Do you believe that your sins are in the past?

Prayer: *Lord I thank You for forgiving me and making me clean and whole. Please help me not to fall back into the trap of guilt and second-guessing. Help me to trust the plan You have for my life and trust that You will be there to guide me every step of the way.*

---

2. *https://m.facebook.com/PassionTranslation/posts/1069636986447815*

5

"The people that walked in darkness have seen a great light; on the inhabitants of a country in shadow dark as death light has blazed forth. You have enlarged the nation, you have increased its joy; they rejoice before you as people rejoice at harvest time, as they exult when they are dividing the spoils. For the yoke that weighed on it, the bar across its shoulders, the rod of its oppressor these you have broken as on the day of Midian. For all the footgear clanking over the ground and all the clothing rolled in blood, will be burnt, will be food for the flames." Isaiah 9:1-4 (NJB)

This prophecy of things to come can be applied to our own lives. During your relationship, you were in the dark. You were confused, frightened and may have even longed for death. But the Lord shone His light into your darkness and called you out of it. He lifted the yoke of your oppressor. He released you from your chains, from your servitude. And He did this not with hesitancy, but with great joy and delight for your freedom.

He mourned with you when you mourned. He felt your pain and your confusion. Having lived a human life, Jesus understands what it feels like to be lied to, lied about, mistreated and abused.

Now Jesus rejoices with you that you are free. If you are second-guessing your decision, know that He does not want you to walk back into the darkness, He does not want you to re-yoke yourself in oppression, and He does not want you to put those bloody clothes back on. Turn your face forward, that's where He is. Let Him lead you forward, not backwards. Embrace your freedom today.

"So if the Son sets you free, you will be free indeed." John 8:36 (NIV)

Reflection: What does it mean to you to stop looking back and only look forward?

Prayer: *Thank You Jesus for my freedom. Guard my heart from the fear or shame that might make we want to turn back. Help me to keep my eyes on You, my mind on you and my heart set on you. Protect me from the enemy's lies. Seal me safe in my freedom!*

6

"For a son has been born for us, a son has been given to us, and dominion has been laid on his shoulders; and this is the name he has been given, 'Won-der-Counsellor, Mighty-God, Eternal-Father, Prince-of-Peace' to extend his dominion in boundless peace, over the throne of David and over his kingdom to make it secure and sustain it in fair judgement and integrity. From this time onwards and for ever, the jealous love of Yahweh Sabaoth will do this." Isaiah 9:5-6 (NJB)

Boundless peace. Can you imagine? One of the most important things you have lost over the course of your relationship is your sense of peace. You may feel as though you will never reclaim it. It feels nebulous, unreachable. You may have panic and or anxiety attacks. You may have nightmares. An innocuous text or email from your former partner might trigger you. Your heart might race, your mind might be overwhelmed with circular thoughts. But Jesus is the Prince-of-Peace! Peace is a part of His Name. Peace is who He is. Philippians 4:7 talks about a peace that doesn't make any sense. That is the peace of Jesus. His peace can penetrate through all of our anxieties and fears.

How do you get that peace? Sit in His Presence, invite Him in. Read your favorite verses aloud, play worship music and sing. Healing comes through time in His presence, the only place where authentic peace can be found. It takes practice. It takes discipline. Sometimes you will have to fight for it. You will need to claim it. But the Prince of Peace is there, waiting for you. Reach for Him today.

"Perfect, absolute peace surrounds those whose imaginations are consumed with you; they confidently trust in you." Isaiah 26:3 (TPT)

Reflection: Are you able to comprehend this peace that the Lord has promised? What is standing in the way?

Prayer: *Jesus, Prince of Peace, let me experience the fullness of your peace. Surround me with your presence and cast out all my fear! Teach me how to walk with You in constant surrounding peace.*

7

"Then the wolf will be subdued and live with the gentle lamb, and the leopard will lie down with the gentle lamb. The young calf and the ferocious lion will be together, and as a shepherd drives his flock, a small child will guide them along! The cow and the bear will graze alongside each other cubs and calves will lie down together. The lion, like the ox, will eat straw. The nursing child will play safely near the rattlesnake's den, and the toddler will stretch out his hand and shine light over the serpent. On all my holy mountain of Zion, nothing evil or harmful will be found. For the earth will be filled with the intimate knowledge of the Lord Yahweh just as water swells the sea!" Isaiah 11:6-9 (TPT)

There are some days when you simply cannot find hope here on Earth. You are overwhelmed; by your pain, by your fears, by the magnitude of energy required to end a relationship. It is challenging to try to disentangle from someone you once loved. Everything is dark around you and you feel alone. On those days you need to take your focus off what is happening here on Earth, and reflect on what Heaven will be like:

No more pain, only freedom.
No more fear, only peace.
No more anxiety, only hope.
No more strife, only joy.
No more enemies, only friends.
No more lies, only truth.

Yes, it is true-one day you *will* leave this all behind you and it will affect you no longer. When you cannot get past what is happening in your current life, think about the one to come. Imagine all of the beautiful and wonderful things that will be there. Make a list of some of the simple things you are looking forward to-no more cleaning, no more bad smells, no more lists of things to do. Reflect on the peace and joy that is coming, while recognizing the value of the life God has given you for now, along with the peace that He offers in the meantime.

"Those Yahweh has set free
will return to Zion and come celebrating with songs of joy!
They will be crowned with never-ending joy!
Gladness and joy will overwhelm them;
despair and depression will disappear!" Isaiah 51:11 (TPT)

Reflection: What are the things on Earth that you are looking forward to leaving behind someday?

Prayer: *Jesus, thank You that Heaven is my true home. Thank You for preparing a place that is so incredible that I cannot imagine it. Help me today to focus on what is to come and to not be focused on the pain of the present.*

" I shall have faith and not be afraid, for Yahweh is my strength and my song, he has been my salvation.' Joyfully you will draw water from the springs of salvation." Isaiah 12: 2b-3 (NJB)

Yahweh is the name the Israelites used for God. Yahweh is your strength. Yahweh is your song. The Bible is filled with songs sung to the Lord; like the songs of Moses, Miriam, David, and Mary. Singing is one of the primary ways that we worship. When we fix our minds on the Lord and sing praises to Him, so many things happen. The enemy cannot stand the sound of our praise, so he flees. We enter into the throne room of the Most High. He meets us there and gives us peace and hope and healing. There are days when you will have to fight for this, days you will have to sing and sing and sing before the breakthrough comes. But persevere! Sing louder, sing longer. Turn the music on high and feel free to express your worship the way that feels most comfortable to you. It might be that you kneel, that you dance, that you prostrate yourself before the Lord, that you wave your hands high. You might do all of those things. If you are comfortable with it, go off book and make up your own words of praise. Psalm 96:1 (NIV) says, "Sing to the LORD a new song; sing to the LORD, all the earth." There is so much healing that comes as we worship, as we open up our hearts to the Healer. He loves to hear the sound of our praises and He

She is Free Indeed

always warmly welcomes us into His Presence.

*"Sing praises to the Lord, for he has done marvelous wonders,
and let his fame be known throughout the earth!
Give out a shout of cheer;
sing for joy, O people of Zion,
for great and mighty is the Holy One of Israel
who lives among you!" Isaiah 12:5-6 (TPT)*

Reflection: Why do you think there is so much power in praise?

Prayer: *Lord, I come into Your presence with singing. Take me into Your holy place so that I can sing Your praise with delight in my heart. Heal my soul as I open it up to You.*

9

In that glorious day, you will say to one another,
"Give thanks to the Lord and ask him for more!
Tell the world about all that he does!
Let them know how magnificent he is!" Isaiah 12:4 (TPT)

"Tell the world what He has done." Revelation 12:11a reads, "They triumphed over him by the blood of the Lamb and by the word of their testimony." "Him," refers to the enemy. There is power in your words. There is power in your story. Part of overcoming the power the enemy has asserted over you via your abusive partner is telling your story of freedom and redemption. It may feel too soon to share, but I would encourage you to begin writing your story and to try to find a support group where you can be heard and supported. Your local women's resource center or community center should have programs like these. If not, there are many online support groups. If you have supportive friends and family it might be good to start sharing with them. You will find that you will meet other women with similar stories. Statistics say that 1/4 and 1/3 of all women will at one point be involved in an abusive relationship. Those other women need to hear your story of deliverance and freedom. Make no mistake about it, it is the Lord who has set you free. Jesus revealed to you that you were in prison and He opened the prison door and called you out. He released you from your chains and you are free. The more you speak that truth, the more power you will take back.

She is Free Indeed

*"Sing praises to the Lord, for he has done marvelous wonders,
and let his fame be known throughout the earth!
Isaiah 12:5 (TPT)*

Reflection: What hope do you think you could offer to women who are still suffering in abusive relationships?

Prayer: *Thank You, Lord, for the power of my testimony. Give me the courage to share it.*

10

"Hold a council, make a decision. At noon spread your shadow as if it were night. Hide those who have been driven out, do not betray the fugitive, let those who have been driven out of Moab come and live with you; be their refuge in the face of the devastator. Once the oppression is past, and the devastation has stopped and those now trampling on the country have gone away, the throne will be made secure in faithful love and on it will sit in con-stancy within the tent of David, a judge seeking fair judgement and pursuing uprightness."
Isaiah 16:4-5

These verses refer to God's judgement toward Moab for its oppressive rule over the Israelites. However, you personally know what it is like to be trampled on by the proud. You know what it is to cry out for justice. You know the devastation of someone trying to tear you apart. But now you get to know the One who sits enthroned in your life with only love. The Lord is constant. His feelings for you do not change. He deals with you fairly. His love is ever faithful. You know what the opposite of this feels and looks like. You lived with it.

So now let the One who has loved you from conception, the One who has watched over you all of your days, the One who loves and adores you be the One you fix your eyes upon. He wants you to hide in the shelter of his wings. He wants you to be completely free. He wants to help you escape the tentacles of fear that still hold you in their grasp. He does not want you to look backwards. He wants you to reach forward, to reach for Him; to let Him embrace you and heal your wounds.

" In that day, people will gaze toward their Creator, and their eyes will look in faith toward the Holy One of Israel. Isaiah 17:7 (TPT)

Reflection: What would you like to ask the Lord for healing for today?

Prayer: *Lord, help me to keep my eyes fixed on You, seeking You for healing rather than looking back at the past. Thank You for my freedom, thank You that You are a just and loving father. Thank You that you will always be faithful to me.*

11

"Lord Yahweh, you are my glorious God!
I will exalt you and praise your name forever,
for you have done so many wonderful things.
Well-thought-out plans you formed in ages past;
you've been faithful and true to fulfill them all!" Isaiah 25:1 (TPT)

When God created the world, He gave us the gift of free will. He also chose not to crush His enemy right away. The results of that are a mixed blessing. We have ultimate freedom in our choices. Sometimes we make mistakes that have a negative impact on our lives. The enemy is out to steal, kill and destroy. It was not God's plan for you to be in an abusive relationship. You may have married someone who seemed to be a devoted Christian. This may have been a front, or things may have happened (such as debilitating accidents, PTSD, or abuse as a child) that changed that man. Whatever the reasons were, it was not God's will for you to be abused.

God does not often give us the answer to the "why?" questions that we ask. But He does tell us:

Who? Christ Himself
What? Working out your healing and redemption
When? Now and in eternity
Where? Heaven is our eternal home.

She is Free Indeed

His ultimate plan which was well thought out and formed in ages past is for you to have communion with Him both now and in eternity. No matter what happens here on Earth, Jesus holds the outcome, He gets the final say. He is faithful to bring about His ultimate goal.

"He wants everyone to be saved and reach full knowledge of the truth."
2 Timothy 2:4 (NJB)

Reflection: What is one thing that you could trust the Lord with today? Can you let go of your need to know the why?

Prayer: *Thank You, Jesus, that You have good plans for me. Thank You that You are not the cause of the horrible things that happen on this earth. Thank You for working in me and that You will continue to work in me until I get to see You face to face!*

12

"For you have been a refuge for the weak, a refuge for the needy in distress, a shelter from the storm, shade from the heat; for the breath of the pitiless is like a winter storm." Isaiah 25:4 (NJB)

Whether we had a happy childhood or a difficult childhood, the Lord has been with us. I met someone once who had been an orphan in India before being adopted by an American family. He told me that even though he was only around 2 years old when he was adopted, he still remembers hearing the Lord speak to him while he was in the orphanage. From a tiny child he had known the Lord. I know a woman who did not come from a Christian family, but she remembers playing on the swings as a preschooler, talking to Jesus.

While God is referred to as a father, He has a mother's heart as well. He has to, otherwise He couldn't have given mothers the hearts they have for their children. He wants to be the One you run to first. He wants to be the place where you hide. He wants to heal you from the harsh things your partner said and did to you. When we take refuge in Him, He heals our wounds. There is no better place, no better program than His Presence for healing and redemption.

She is Free Indeed

"The name of the LORD is a fortified tower; the righteous run to it and are safe." Proverbs 18:10 (NLT)

Reflection: What are the qualities of a good mother? What are the qualities of a good father? Are you able to see those in the Lord?

Prayer: *Lord, thank You for being my safe place. Thank You that You are always waiting, with arms wide open, to hold me close. Help me to run to You when I need refuge and trust that You are always there.*

13

"On this mountain, for all peoples, Yahweh Sabaoth is preparing a banquet of rich food, a banquet of fine wines, of succulent food, of well-strained wines. On this mountain, he has destroyed the veil which used to veil all peoples, the pall enveloping all nations; he has destroyed death for ever. Lord Yahweh has wiped away the tears from every cheek; he has taken his people's shame away everywhere on earth, for Yahweh has spoken."
Isaiah 25:6-8 (NJB)

The Lord has good things in store for you. While this passage refers more specifically to Heaven, we know that the Kingdom of God is here on Earth already. While we do not yet experience its fullness, we can experience it in part. He has already won the victory over sin and death. He has already removed your shame. One day soon, He will wipe all the tears from your eyes and the veil that divides Heaven from Earth will be lifted.

As you enter the Lord's presence, as you climb up the mountain of the Lord, do so with thanksgiving for all that He has done and all that He will do. Know that while you are still suffering here on earth, He is preparing your place in eternity and He delights in doing so. Yes, you will still suffer here; it's unavoidable. But keep reminding yourself of the glory that is to come, the feast that the Lord is preparing. He waits with even more anticipation than we do, because He knows the richness and fullness of what will be. He is longing to know you more. He is longing for you to see Him face to face. Though our eyes are still veiled on this earth, He gives us glimpses of Himself. Seek His face, and in Him your longings will be fulfilled.

"My heart says of you, "Seek his face!" o&r face, LORD, I will seek." Psalm 27:8 (NIV)

Reflection: Take a moment and imagine what paradise would look like for you. Reflect on the fact that what God has in store for you is infinitely more incredible.

Prayer: *Thank You, Lord for the place You are preparing for me. Help me to seek Your face with all of my heart so that I might experience your presence here on Earth.*

14

"And on that day, it will be said, 'Look, this is our God, in him we put our hope that he should save us, this is Yahweh, we put our hope in him. Let us exult and rejoice since he has saved us.' For Yahweh's hand will rest on this mountain." Isaiah 25:9-10a (NJB)

In this passage, *"that day"* is referring to the end of time. How many times has the Lord ordained that day for you? There are many times in our lives when the Lord steps in on a certain day in a powerful way and He brings us freedom, deliverance, healing, and peace.

The Lord ordained, *"that day"* that you walked away from your abusive partner. He was there in a mighty way that day, whether you felt Him or not. He was proud of you for stepping away from that destruction, He was delighted in you for your faith. And now every day, that power and strength is available to you. His hand rests upon you. The promises that He made to you that day are still true. He didn't take his hand off you once you were free. He didn't take his attention from you either. He is still *that close*. He is always waiting to rescue you. He is always waiting to hold you close. In the fear and the darkness, cry out to Him. When you are confused and distressed, open His word to hear His promises.

She is Free Indeed

*"This is the day the Lord has made;
We will rejoice and be glad in it."* Psalm 118:24 (NKJV)

Reflection: What "days,' are you believing the Lord for in the future?

Prayer: *Lord, I thank You that today is Your day. Help me to learn what you want me to learn today. Help me to trust that You are with me at all times.*

15

*"Perfect, absolute peace surrounds those
whose imaginations are consumed with you;
they confidently trust in you.
Yes, trust in the Lord Yahweh forever and ever!
For Yah, the Lord God, is your Rock of Ages!" Isaiah 26:3-5 (TPT)*

You may remember the opening words to the old hymn, "Rock of ages cleft for Me, let me hide myself in thee." What does it mean that He is the Rock of Ages? Psalm 118:22 (NIV) prophetically refers to Jesus, "The stone the builders rejected has become the cornerstone."

Jesus is our rock. He is our place of safety. He is the only place where, "perfect, absolute peace," can be found. The Bible is full of references to our God, the rock. An earthly rock may be broken or crushed, but God cannot. What does it mean for our, "imaginations," to be consumed with the Lord? The Word in Hebrew is *sa-muk*, and it is only used one other time in the Bible. It means, "to lay, lean, rest and support." To have that peace, we have to constantly work to keep our minds leaned on and resting in the support of the Lord. It is not a natural state, it is often one we must fight for. Sometimes it is easier than others. When we are trying to keep something steady, there is a constant awareness and attention needed. This takes practice. No one gets up on a balance beam and is able to balance right away. It takes hours and hours of practice and still some of the best gymnasts in the world fall sometimes.

"Therefore thus says the Lord GOD, "Behold, I am laying in Zion a stone, a tested stone, A costly cornerstone for the foundation, firmly placed. He who believes in it will not be disturbed." Isaiah 28:16 (NASB)

Reflection: What are some things that distract you from the Lord's presence? What are some simple things you could do to alleviate these distractions?

Prayer: *Jesus, keep my mind steadily on You. Help me to keep a constant awareness of Your presence so that I can access the perfect peace You offer. Help me to remember to seek You first each day.*

16

"The path of the righteous is smooth and level;
God, the Just One, you make a clear path for them.
Yes, we will follow your ways, Lord Yahweh,
and entwine our hearts with yours,
for the fame of your name is all that we desire.
At night I yearn for you with all my heart;
in the morning my spirit reaches out to you." Isaiah 26:7-9a
(TPT)

Reading the words, "The path of the righteous is smooth and level," you might have rolled your eyes, or at least raised your eyebrows. I am sure that your path has been anything but smooth or level. What I believe this passage is referring to is that as you seek to glorify and honor the Lord, He will make His way and His plans for you clear. But we must entwine our hearts with His. How do we do that when our traumatized brains don't allow us to focus on anything for any length of time?

First, we must decide, is "the fame of your name," all that we desire? Have we decided to put the Lord and His purposes for us first? Is He the object of our foremost desire? If so, then we have a starting point. He loves to answer our prayers when we ask him to help us to yearn more for Him. And as we practice, we build up those spiritual muscles so that He is the first thing we think about in the morning and the One to whom we cry in the night.

She is Free Indeed

You might be able to concentrate for less than a minute right now. That's ok. As you persevere, you will build your ability to focus on the Lord. And the more you focus on Him, the clearer your path becomes.

"He guides me in the paths of righteousness For His name's sake." Psalm 23:3b (ESV)

Reflection: What does the phrase, "the fame of your name," mean to you?

Prayer: *Lord teach me to seek You and find You so that I may know the steps You want me to take. Help me to keep my eyes fixed on You.*

17

"Yahweh, you will grant us peace, having completed all our undertakings for us. Yahweh our God, other lords than you have ruled us but, loyal to you alone, we invoke your name." Isaiah 26:12-13 (NJB)

The Passion Translation translates these verses as, "All that we accomplish is the result of what you work through us." Other translations of these verses interpret this passage as either the Lord working on our behalf or working through us to accomplish His will. Whatever translation you prefer, ultimately, the glory goes to the Lord.

He is the one who worked to set you free from your destructive relationship. He is the one who lit the path ahead of you when you walked out of darkness.

When you were in that abusive relationship, another lord ruled you. Your partner worked very hard to exert power and control over you. He wanted you under his dominion and authority. There is no such thing as peace in such a situation.

The only one who should have any authority over you is Jesus Christ. And He never exerts his authority over us, or dominates us. Instead He leads us gently when we call on his name. And He leads us into his peace. Peace comes from knowing that you are following your Saviour on the path that He has set before you.

Then Jesus came to them and said, "All authority in Heaven and on earth has been given to me." Matthew 28:18 (NIV)

Reflection: What does it mean to you to give authority to Jesus today?

Prayer: *Thank You, Jesus for leading me out from the authority of darkness and into Your great light. I want You to lead me and guide my steps. I surrender to Your authority alone.*

18

"But your dead will live again! Their bodies will rise from the dead! It's time to awaken and sing for joy, you dwellers in the dust! As the glistening, radiant dew refreshes the earth, so the Lord will awaken those dwelling among the dead." Isaiah 26:19 (TPT)

The Bible talks about us being dead in sin and needing the resurrecting power of Jesus to wash away our sin. But there are other ways that someone can be "dead." In your relationship you lost parts of yourself. You lost your identity, you may have lost your mental health, you may have lost friends or been isolated from your family. You were not yourself anymore. But the resurrecting power of Jesus Christ is not just about sin. It is about all of you: soul, mind, spirit and body. We are promised a completely renewed body once we are in Heaven, but in the meantime here on earth, the Lord wants you to live fully. He wants to breathe life back into those areas of your life that were stolen from you.

And once you are, "awake," it is time to sing. It is time to sing the song of your resurrection.

Brooke Ligerwood's beautiful song of praise, Awake, goes,

There is a sound that changes things
The sound of His people on their knees
Oh wake up you slumbering

She is Free Indeed

It's time to worship Him
Awake my soul and sing
Sing His praise aloud
Sing His praise aloud [1]

So, sing your song, glorify the Lord for what He has done.

"Then he said to me, "Prophesy to these bones and say to them, 'Dry bones, hear the word of the Lord! 5 This is what the Sovereign Lord says to these bones: I will make breath enter you, and you will come to life. 6 I will attach tendons to you and make flesh come upon you and cover you with skin; I will put breath in you, and you will come to life. Then you will know that I am the Lord.'" Ezekiel 37:4-6 (NIV)

Reflection: Is your soul awake today? What are the things that lead you to slumber in your relationship with the Lord?

Prayer: *Lord, awaken my soul today. Let me not grow tired of spending time with You. Let me live full of Your life today.*

---

1. Ligertwood, Brooke. Awake. Hillsong Worship. 2019

19

"Then God will supply you with abundant rain for the seeds you sow. He will bless you with an incredible, plentiful harvest. And in that day he will give you lush, broad pastures for your cattle. Even your oxen and don-keys that work the soil will feed on good grain, separated from its chaff. On the day of great slaughter, when all their towers tumble, God will bless you with sparkling streams and bubbling brooks flowing down every high hill and every lofty mountain."
Isaiah 30:23-25 (TPT)

It is so easy to get dragged back into the cycle of fear and anxiety. For a long time, you put your trust in a man who failed you. When trust is so irrevocably broken, you are left open and vulnerable. The enemy loves to get in there and make your thoughts spin, your heart race and your sleep fitful. When those times come it's time to use your sword, the sword of the Spirit which is the word of
God. Open your Bible
and begin to read aloud. It is good to make a list of verses you can turn to when fear trips you up.

The verses above are an excellent example. God is going to supply you, He is going to bless you. New life is going to spring up and your harvest is going to be plentiful. Verse 24 talks about your animals feed-ing on grain that has been winnowed. The Hebrew word is, *zohreh* and is found also in the book of Ruth when Naomi instructs Ruth to go to the threshing floor where Boaz is "winnowing" barley. When Boaz has finished winnowing, he lays down to sleep beside the pile of now pure and clean barley. God does not

She is Free Indeed

want you having to deal with "chaff." He wants you to feed on the pure nourishment that His Word provides. Ruth had come from devastation in Moab to live in poverty in Israel. But poverty was not what the Lord had for her. He had plans to bless her just as in the words of Isaiah above.

Then Jesus declared, "I am the bread of life. Whoever comes to me will never go hungry, and whoever believes in me will never be thirsty." John 6:35 (NIV)

Reflection: Do you believe that the Lord will supply all of your needs? If not, why?

Prayer: *Lord thank You for the wonderful things You have promised me. Help me to step out of my fear and speak Your words of truth and life.*

20

"My people will see the awesome glory of Yahweh, the beautiful grandeur of our God. Strengthen those who are discouraged. Energize those who feel defeated. Say to the anxious and fearful, "Be strong and never afraid. Look, here comes your God! He is breaking through to give you victory! He comes to avenge your enemies. With divine retribution he comes to save you!"
Isaiah 35:2b-4 (TPT)

Extricating yourself from a relationship is usually a very painful and messy process. There have inevitably been lies told about you, and sometimes your own friends and family will have believed them. In these verses the Lord is promising the justice you deserve. He is promising that you will be vindicated. The only problem is that we do not know when that will happen. It may not happen until the Day of the Lord comes and His reckoning takes place. It is difficult to imagine how long you might have to wait. While you are waiting, remember that Jesus is waiting alongside you. Jesus is also waiting for His own vindication in the minds of all who have rejected Him and believed lies about Him. He longs for that day even more than you do.

We indeed have a Saviour who is familiar with our suffering. There is little of humanity that He did not experience in His sojourn on this earth. You are not alone. He is standing there right beside you. Your vindication is coming. Your Saviour is coming. Hold onto him so that He can fill you with His strength.

She is Free Indeed

"For the LORD of hosts will have a day of reckoning against everyone who is proud and lofty And against everyone who is lifted up, That he may be abased." Isaiah 2:12 (NASB)

Reflection: What does it mean to you to know that Jesus feels your suffering as much as you do?

Prayer: *Thank You Lord that my victory and my vindication are on the way. Thank You that You intimately understand and empathize with what I am experiencing. Help me to trust and hold on to You until that day comes.*

🌸 21 🌸

*"Then blind eyes will open and deaf ears will hear
Then the lame will leap like playful deer
and the tongue-tied will sing songs of triumph.
Gushing water will spring up in the wilderness
and streams will flow through the desert.
The burning sand will become a refreshing oasis.*

Isaiah 35:5-7a (NASB)

These verses immediately follow the ones from the previous reading. These are promises that are "already, but not yet." These are things you can experience in part today, knowing that you will experience them in full once the Lord has come.

Your eyes were blinded when you were being abused. Your ears were unable to hear truths. You were crippled in spirit and you lost your voice. You were in a dark and frightening place. You walked as though on hot coals or eggshells. Your spirit was dry and your home was truly a "dragon's lair."

Now, the Lord wants you to see all of His beauty in the world, in His creation, in the people around you and in Himself. He wants you to be able to hear and know what is true. He wants your spirit to come alive again with joy in His presence. He wants you to experience His rivers of life flowing out of you! He wants you to be able to walk His path in confidence and peace. And he definitely wants you to stay away from that dragon's lair. He does not want you going back there, physically, mentally or emotionally. Hold on to these truths!

"Now on the last day, the great day of the feast, Jesus stood and cried out, saying, "If anyone is thirsty, let him come to Me and drink. He who believes in Me, as the Scripture said, 'From his innermost being will flow rivers of living water.'" John 7:37-38 (NASB)

Reflection: What would it look like to have "rivers of living water," flowing from you?

Prayer: *Thank You Jesus for Your promises. Help me to walk in the fullness of what I can experience here on this earth. Let Your life flow through all of me.*

22

"For those whom Yahweh has ransomed will return, they will come to Zion shouting for joy, their heads crowned with joy unending; rejoicing and glad-ness will escort them and sorrow and sighing will take flight."
Isaiah 35:10 (NJB)

According to the dictionary, a ransom is, "the redemption of a prisoner, slave, or kidnapped person, of captured goods, etc., for a price." While the Bible refers to Jesus paying the ransom for our sin, this verse can also be applied to your abusive relationship. While your body may or may not have been kidnapped, your soul was. It could even be argued that you stayed as long as you did because you developed something like Stockholm Syndrome, an unhealthy psychological bond with your abuser.

Now that your ransom has been paid, now that Jesus has set you free, it's time to shout for joy, it's time to speak praise and to sing praise. The longest book in the Bible is the book of Psalms. As you read through the Psalms you will find a prayer/song that applies to every part of the human experience. Read through them until you find one that applies to you today and then pray it aloud. Whatever lies behind you or before you, give praise to the Lord for ransoming you. You may want to praise Him with words like these, "I will exalt you, LORD, for you rescued me. You refused to let my enemies triumph over me." Psalm 31:1 (NLT)

She is Free Indeed

"But I trust in your unfailing love. I will rejoice because you have rescued me." Psalm 13:5 (NLT)

Reflection: Reflect on the journey the Lord has taken you on thus far. Think of specific things you can praise Him for today, and then do it.

Prayer: *Thank You Jesus for paying my ransom and redeeming me from the enemy's grasp. I want to praise You all of my days and sing of all You have done for me!*

❋ 23 ❋

"When King Hezekiah's ministers came to Isaiah, he said to them, 'Say to your master, "Yahweh says this: Do not be afraid of the words which you have heard or the blasphemies which the king of Assyria's minions have uttered against me." "Look, I am going to put a spirit in him and, on the strength of a rumour, he will go back to his own country, and in that country I shall make him fall by the sword." Isaiah 37:6-7 (NJB)

Words are the most powerful weapons we have, both for good and evil. You know intimately the harm your partner's words caused you. With time, you will probably remember even more. And just because you have left doesn't mean that he will stop his verbal assaults. And in many cases, it may get worse as he works hard to make himself look like the victim and you look crazy.

In the passage above, Judah was under siege by Assyria. They were surrounded on all sides and desperately afraid. Yet Isaiah the prophet sent a message from the Lord to King Hezekiah that he should not be afraid of the threats from the king of Assyria. This must have seemed absurd. Judah was completely overpowered, there was no rational reason to hope. But Hezekiah knew the Lord. He knew God's promises were true. Was he still a little bit afraid? Probably. But he put his trust in God's message to him, that the king of Assyria's words meant nothing. And God did what He promised to do.

She is Free Indeed

Hide yourself in the Father's arms when you hear the things being said about you, when you receive distressing and threatening messages from your former partner and his family and friends. Cling to the hope that only the word of the Lord will stand in the end.

"He rescues me unharmed from the battle waged against me, even though many oppose me." Psalm 55:18 (NIV)

Reflection: What are some specific lies that have been said about you that you can bring before the Lord today? Ask Him to help you to heal and to reveal the truth of your character to you.

Prayer: *Lord please guard my heart from the words that come like arrows against me. Help me to put my trust in You alone and in Your promises for me.*

24

"...Do not let the God on whom you are relying deceive you..."
Isaiah 37: 10 (NJB)

If your former partner claims to be a Christian it is very likely that he used both God and the Bible against you many times. And now that you have left, he may accuse you of turning your back on God. And unfortunately, others will as well. You may find many who will quote the Bible in an attempt to show you the error of your ways. They will tell you that you weren't submissive enough, that you should have respected him more. They will tell you that God hates divorce. Indeed, he does, but the verse used to support this idea is from Malachi 2:16. This verse references the divorce where a man abandons his wife. Women did not have the right to divorce in Biblical times. It could be argued, therefore, that God hates abuse more than he hates divorce. He tells us, in Proverbs 3:23 (NIV) "Above all else, guard your heart, for everything you do flows from it."

If your partner claims to be a Christian he may enter a hyper-religious phase where he will do anything to convince those around him that he is the victim, not you. He will question your faith and others may as well.

Hold on to the promises you've been given. You are ultimately accountable to the Most High, not to anyone on earth. Rely on your God! You alone know your relationship with Him! He is true and He is just and He is faithful.

*"Many are saying of me,
"God will not deliver (David) him."
But you, Lord, are a shield around me, my
glory, the One who lifts my head high. I call
out to the Lord,
and he answers me from his holy mountain."
Psalm 3:2- 4 (NIV)*

Reflection: What lies were you told that kept you in that relationship? Ask the Lord to counter those with the truth for you today.

Prayer: *Thank You, Lord, that You are a loving Father, that You took me away from the one who was harming me. Thank You that when others don't see the truth, I know I have the truth in You. Help me to remember this.*

❃ 25 ❃

"You will cure me. Restore me to life. At once, my bitterness turns to well-being. For you have preserved my soul from the pit of nothingness, you have thrust all my sins behind you. For Sheol cannot praise you, nor Death celebrate you; those who go down to the pit can hope no longer in your constancy. The living, the living are the ones who praise you, as I do today."
Isaiah 38:16b-19a (NJB)

Holding onto bitterness is like holding onto the grave itself. If you hold onto it, you keep yourself in the pit, in the dungeon and your soul will decay. You will not be truly free.

Letting go of your bitterness and forgiving is one of the most challenging things the Lord asks us to do. The thought of it can be overwhelming, especially if you have endured decades of abuse. Generally, it does not all come at once, but in phases as the Lord leads. There is no quick fix (although the Lord does do miracles.) The important thing is recognizing where your heart is at. Do you want to forgive? Do you want to let go of your bitterness? Or are you ruminating on all that your former partner did to you?

Come before the Lord in prayer. Imagine yourself at the foot of His cross, receiving forgiveness for all that you have done. While in general it is not a good idea to bring to mind your past sins if you have already repented and received forgiveness for them, in this case reflecting on all that you have been forgiven for is a good thing. As you remember, then picture your former partner at the foot of the cross. While he might not actually be there himself, Jesus paid the punishment for his sin against you on the cross that day as well. At the foot of the cross, we are all the same: broken sinners needing grace.

"And forgive us our debts, as we also have forgiven our debtors."
Matthew 6:12 (NIV)

Reflection: Where are you at with forgiveness today? Is it too big to consider? Ask the Lord to guide you gently on this path.

Prayer: *Thank You Lord, that You have never hesitated to forgive me. Help me on my path out of bitterness and into forgiveness. Protect my heart on this healing path.*

26

*"He will care for you as a shepherd tends his flock,
gathering the weak lambs and taking them in his arms.
He carries them close to his heart
and gently leads those that have young."*
Isaiah 40:11 (TPT)

Are you close to the Father's heart? Do you allow Him to gently lead you? Biblically, a husband is supposed to love his wife like Christ loved the church and lay himself down for her. Having even one man you are close to so poorly represent the Lord can be devastating. Many of you may have had fathers who did a poor job as well. It can become extremely difficult to relate to the Lord as a man or as a father given the terrible examples you may have had.

If you know anything about sheep you know they aren't very bright and they are tremendously skittish. I have seen full grown sheep run away in fear from a tiny baby goat. A shepherd has to be the gentlest of humans. A shepherd must have a lot of patience and cannot have emotional swings in view of the sheep. A shepherd understands that sheep react according to their limited understanding and therefore treats them very gently and speaks very softly.

Can you picture the Lord like this? He is the safest harbor you will ever find. He wants to hold you close to His heart and He wants to gently lead you. Will you let Him?

*"The Lord is my shepherd,
I shall not want.
He makes me lie down in green pastures;
He leads me beside quiet waters.
He restores my soul;"*
Psalm 23:1-2 (NASB)

Reflection: Does the word, "father," trigger negative feelings for you? Consider using another name for God, like *Abba*, the Hebrew word for father.

Prayer: *Lord please remove the negative images of men and fathers from my perception of You. Help me to trust that you will be gentle and tender-hearted with me as I come to You.*

27

The Holy One asks, "Can you find anyone or anything to compare to Me? Where is the one equal to me?" Isaiah 40:25 (TPT)

It is so easy in our pain to turn to the temporarily satisfying things the world has to offer. It may be sugar or other foods, TV or movies, alcohol, drugs, sex or other things than can be addicting. The problem with those things is that while they soothe us for a little while, the good feeling does not last, nor is it healthy.

It is incredibly difficult to break those habits because they all cause the neurotransmitters in your brain to do a happy dance, fooling you into believing that they really do make things better. You often feel worse after over-eating, drinking too much or indulging in something that numbs your brain. You continue to fall for the tricks of those bad habits again and again because you crave that release of pleasure, no matter how fleeting it is.

In her book, *Made to Crave*, Lysa TerKeurst writes, "God made us to crave—to desire eagerly, want greatly, and long for Him. But Satan wants to do everything possible to replace our craving for God with something else."[1] The only thing that will ever soothe us deep in our souls is our relationship with Jesus. When you get a craving for those temporal, unhealthy vices,

---

1. Thomas Nelson, 2010

run to Him first. Let Him soothe your soul

*"O God, you are my God; earnestly I seek you;
my soul thirsts for you; my flesh faints for you,
as in a dry and weary land where there is no water."*
Psalm 63:1 (ESV)

Reflection: Make a list of the things you crave. What are some healthier alternatives?

Prayer: *Lord, when I am needy, help me to remember to run to You first. Help me to find the peace and the satiation of Your presence and Your healing touch.*

*If you feel like something that you are using to ease your negative feelings is becoming a habit, please consider reaching out for help from community services in your area or an organization such as Alcoholics Anonymous.

28

"So mighty is His power, so great is His strength." Isaiah 40:26b (NJB)

Abusers assert power over their victims. They want their victims to feel powerless. They steal their voices. They want absolute control. It is very difficult to come out from under that. When you leave, the abuser does not stop trying to assert their false authority over you. They may try even harder. You may find yourself strongly emotionally triggered by the simplest of things: a text, an email, or even a look. When you need to reply or to act on it, you are pushed right back into the fear cycle. There are two strong adjectives and two nouns used in the passage above to describe God. His "power" is "mighty," and his "strength" is "great." Remember who your God is. He is the creator of the universe; the one who holds all time and history in His hands. I encourage you to read Job 38 and 39 today. It is a powerful passage where God speaks of His own might and power. He is bigger and stronger than any man, any lawyer, any judge, any pastor. Held side by side in the balances, they disappear. That power is there for you today. He is on your side. Whatever may happen, He will be with you at all times.

She is Free Indeed

"Where were you when I laid the earth's foundations? Tell me, since you are so well-informed! Who decided its dimensions, do you know? Or who stretched the measuring line across it? What supports its pillars at their bases? Who laid its cornerstone to the joyful concert of the morning stars and unanimous acclaim of the sons of God?" Job 38:4-7 (NJB)

Reflection: What does it mean to know that the Lord is infinitely more powerful than your former partner ever was?

Prayer: *Lord, break off the power my former partner had over me. I submit to Your authority alone. Help me to remember how powerful and mighty You are when I am afraid. Help me to always trust You.*

29

"He gives strength to the weary, he strengthens the powerless. Youths grow tired and weary, the young stumble and fall, but those who hope in Yahweh will regain their strength, they will sprout wings like eagles, though they run they will not grow weary, though they walk they will never tire."
Isaiah 40:29-31 (NJB)

In the previous devotional, we read about God's power and how He uses it to keep us safe. In these verses we read of the offer He makes to give that power to us.

You are, no doubt, exhausted and feeling powerless. You were supposed to be under the Lord's authority so that He could give you strength and hope, but a man inserted himself into your life to usurp that authority. Now that you are free, it is time to run back to the Lord, to allow Him to give you back the power He offers.

Throughout this healing process you will likely fall many times. You are not perfect and your brain has been affected by the trauma which means that your reactions will often be over the top. That is normal, it is ok. The Lord will pick you up again so that you can continue on your journey. You may not be ready to run yet, but the time will come. And once you are running, you may not be able to imagine sprouting wings and flying, but that too is on God's agenda for you. Stay the course. Keep seeking Him.

She is Free Indeed

On difficult days fall at His feet and let Him give you His strength.

"The LORD is my strength and my shield; my heart trusts in him, and he helps me. My heart leaps for joy, and with my song I praise him."
Psalm 28:7 (NIV)

Reflection: What does it mean to you to know that the Lord's power is more than enough for you today?

Prayer: *Thank You that You are the true head of my soul. Thank You that you never fail. Please give me Your strength and hope today. May the truth set me free.*

30

"You are my servant, I have chosen you, I have not rejected you,' 10.do not be afraid, for I am with you; do not be alarmed, for I am your God. I give you strength, truly I help you, truly I hold you firm with my saving right hand." Isaiah 41:9b-10 (NJB)

Know today that the Lord is the direct opposite of your former partner. Your partner did choose you, but he chose you as a target. He chose you because he thought he could take your power away from you and exert his own authority over you. He fed your fear, he took your strength. He rejected the good and beautiful things about you.

It is difficult to trust after such a deeply traumatic season. But you can always trust the Lord, who chose you. Yes, you! He will never reject you or turn His back on you. He will never condemn you or call you names or get frustrated and give up on you. He wants you to rest in his safety. He wants you to know that He holds your soul firmly in the palm of His hand, but also tenderly, like someone would hold a baby bird, His other hand on top of you, sheltering you. He doesn't want to be an after thought. He wants you to be aware of His presence and care every moment of every day.

Brother Lawrence, in, The Practice of the Presence of God, writes, "That we need only to recognize GOD intimately present with us, to address ourselves to Him every moment, that we may beg His assistance for knowing His will in things doubtful, and for rightly performing those which we plainly see He requires of us, offering them to Him before we do them, and giving Him thanks when we have done."[1]

"The life of every living thing is in His hand, as well as the breath of all mankind." Job 12:10 (BSB)

Reflection: Make a list of all of the ways that the Lord is the opposite of what your partner was.

Prayer: *Thank You Lord that You are a good Father. Thank You that You only bring me good things. Thank You for Your protection. Help me to always run to You first.*

---

1. Whitaker House. 1982

31

"Here is my servant whom I uphold, my chosen one in whom my soul delights. I have sent my spirit upon him, he will bring fair judgement to the nations. He does not cry out or raise his voice, his voice is not heard in the street; he does not break the crushed reed or snuff the faltering wick. Faithful-ly he presents fair judgement;" Isaiah 42:1-3

I remember reading these verses as a child and being struck by the tenderness of Jesus that is portrayed by them. The NLT reads, "He will not crush the weakest reed or put out a flickering candle." It meant so much to me, even then. When you have experienced the trauma of abuse, you are indeed the weakest reed, your candle is dim. You have been crushed, you have been persecuted, you have felt abandoned. Jesus says, "It is not the healthy who need a doctor, but the sick." (Mark 2:7 NIV). Psalm 34:18 states: "The Lord is close to the broken-hearted and saves those who are crushed in spirit" (NIV).

The Bible is full of these references. Over and over, we see the tenderness of God. Too often He is viewed as full of judgment and vengeance. If your own father was not loving, you have probably struggled to see God as loving. But He cries out so many times that He has come to heal and to love and to give life. Jesus is the only safe place. What is fair is only found in Him. He will strengthen the crushed reed and He will breathe on the flickering candle so that it can flare once more.

She is Free Indeed

"We are hard pressed on every side, but not crushed; perplexed, but not in despair; persecuted, but not abandoned; struck down, but not destroyed." (2 Corinthians 4:8 NIV)

Reflection: Is it difficult for you to imagine the tenderness of God? What is getting in the way of this truth?

Prayer: *Thank You Jesus for Your tender care. I give You the broken and faltering pieces of my soul and ask You to heal them. Knit me back together again as you did as I was in my mother's womb.*

32

"Faithfully he presents fair judgement; 4.he will not grow faint, he will not be crushed until he has established fair judgement on earth, and the coasts and islands are waiting for his instruction." Isaiah 42:3b-4 (NJB)

This is a prophetic reference to Jesus, the coming Messiah who, at the end of time, will wipe injustice off of the face of the planet.

As you disentangle yourself from your former partner you will invariably face injustice. Sadly, true justice is not to be found yet in the here and now. And attempting to find justice for yourself and your children (if you have children) can be incredibly frustrating and soul rending. Unfortunately, lawyers and judges are given no special training to be able to understand the nature of psychological or emotional abuse. Most of them simply do not get it. And your partner will most likely continue to fight you and throw accusations your way.

It is incredibly difficult to accept the fact that you may not find justice on this earth. You may lose and you may lose big. But what you can hold onto is the fact that Jesus is coming again, and this time He will establish perfect and complete justice. You will be fully vindicated. It is coming. Hold onto Him while you wait.

She is Free Indeed

Amos 5:24 (ESV) "But let justice roll down like waters, and righteousness like an ever-flowing stream."

Reflection: Imagine the future today. What will it look and feel like when you are finally vindicated? Praise the Lord that it is going to happen.

> **Prayer:** *Lord I deeply long for justice here and now. Please hold me up and help me to remember that it is coming, and that You are coming. Help me to not fall into despair as I wait for it. Help me to keep my eyes on You.*

33

"I, Yahweh, have called you in saving justice, I have grasped you by the hand and shaped you; I have made you a covenant of the people and light to the nations, 7.to open the eyes of the blind, to free captives from prison, and those who live in darkness from the dungeon. 8.I am Yahweh, that is my name! I shall not yield my glory to another, nor my honour to idols."
Isaiah 42:6-8 (NJB)

Over and over we see these promises of freedom in the Old Testament. There are some theological schools of thought who gauge the significance of a Biblical theme based on how often it appears in the canon of Scripture. If we were to apply that to the topic of justice, it would be deemed extraordinarily important. There are 133 references to the word *mishpat*, which is Hebrew for justice, and 421 references to words derived from *mishpat*. Clearly, justice is near to the Lord's heart.

While we know that we may not see total justice on this side of eternity, we are still prisoners who have been set free! The Lord opened your eyes to see the destructive nature of your relationship, and then He led you out of your prison. Your partner tried to make himself your idol, but the Lord does not yield his glory to another. A true partner would have encouraged you to put Jesus first, above himself. He would have wanted to see Jesus glorified in you. He would have honored the gifts the Lord has given you. It is nearly impossible to reach your potential in

She is Free Indeed

Christ with a voice in your home that constantly demeans and accuses you. Jesus wants you to come into the fulness of what He has for you, now that you have been freed from that prison.

Galatians 5:1 (NIV) "It is for freedom that Christ has set us free. Stand firm, then, and do not let yourselves be burdened again by a yoke of slavery."

Reflection: How could you rejoice over your freedom today? Could you sing, or paint or dance or write?

Prayer: *Thank you Jesus, for saving me. Thank you that I have all freedom in You. Help me to never look back, to never long for the familiarity of my prison cell. Thank You that You are working on justice for me.*

34

"I will walk the blind by an unknown way
and guide them on paths they've never traveled.
I will smooth their difficult road
and make their dark mysteries bright with light.
These are things I will do for them,
for I will never abandon my beloved ones.
17 But those who trust in idols,
who say to their metal images,
"You are our gods,"
will be turned aside in total disgrace."
Isaiah 42:16-17 (TPT)

When you first committed to this relationship, you had complete trust in your new partner. You thought he was going to be your beloved, that he was going to love and support you and that you were going to have a future together.

As time wore on, you became confused. The lies, accusations, manipulation and cruelty blinded you.

Weeks, months, and years before you left you could not have even imagined leaving. The idea was abhorrent. And when you began to consider the idea of leaving, you probably may have had absolutely no idea how you were going to do it. That's when Jesus stepped in and led you out of the darkness. He exposed the abuse in your relationship. You followed Him in obedience as you stepped out of it.

She is Free Indeed

You were never abandoned. You are His beloved. The Lord was always there with you. As you unpack the years of abuse you will increasingly find that the dark memories are lit up. You will begin to make connections and gain understanding. God doesn't show us truth all at once, as that would be too overwhelming. He will show you piece by piece the puzzle of the true picture of your relationship. Trust Him in this process.

"But you are a chosen people, a royal priesthood, a holy nation, God's special possession, that you may declare the praises of him who called you out of darkness into his wonderful light." 1 Peter 2:9 (NIV)

Reflection: What does the Lord use to show you His will? Is it His word? Is it His people? Which can you trust the most?

Prayer: *Thank you Lord that you shine a light in the darkness, that you show me Your truth. Continue to guide me on this new, untrodden path. Help me to follow with trust, knowing You are holding my hand.*

35

Now, this is what Yahweh says:
"Listen, Jacob, to the One who created you,
Israel, to the one who shaped who you are
Do not fear, for I, your Kinsman-Redeemer, will rescue you.
I have called you by name, and you are mine.
Isaiah 43:1 (TPT)

The Passion Translation of this verse (above) uses the term, "Kinsmen Redeemer." In the original Hebrew the word is simply, "redeemed." The only Biblical occurrences in Hebrew of "kinsmen-redeemer" are in the book of Ruth and refer to Boaz, who eventually embraces Ruth as his wife because her husband died. God calls us His children (which makes us kin) but also refers to Himself as a husband to the widow. While your partner may not have died, your relationship did.

Your Heavenly Father shaped you. He called you by name, He claimed you as His. He rescued you, His daughter, and now He wants to meet all of your needs. Are you ready to give Him headship of your life?

Ruth, a widow, left Moab with nothing. She followed her mother-in-law, Naomi, having no idea what lay ahead for her. She chose the God of Israel and threw herself upon his mercy. And he provided Boaz, a kinsmen redeemer for her.

She is Free Indeed

Are you ready to listen? Are you ready to release your fear? You belong to the Lord and He is your protector and defender. Jesus wants to be your kinsmen-redeemer.

Ruth 4:14 (NJB) "And the women said to Naomi, 'Blessed be Yahweh who has not left you today without anyone to redeem you. May his name be praised in Israel!'"

Reflection: How is your journey similar to that of Ruth? Does that give you hope for the future?

Prayer: *Thank you Lord, for being my kinsmen redeemer. Thank you for forming me and rescuing me and meeting all of my needs. I want to give You headship in my life. I want my face to reflect Your glory.*

36

"Should you pass through the waters, I shall be with you; or through rivers, they will not swallow you up. Should you walk through fire, you will not suffer, and the flame will not burn you." Isaiah 43:2 (NJB)

In Daniel 3, the story of Shadrach, Meshach and Abednego is told. They disobeyed the king's directive to bow in worship at his golden idol. The consequence to this is was to be thrown into a blazing furnace. Daniel 3:16-17 (NASB) "The men told the king, "O Nebuchadnezzar, we do not need to give you an answer concerning this matter. If it be so, our God whom we serve is able to deliver us from the furnace of blazing fire; and He will deliver us out of your hand, O king."

Shadrach, Meshach and Abednego were willing to follow God no matter what. God indeed honored their faith and they were not burned up in the furnace, and in fact there was a fourth person in there with them, who looked like, "a son of the gods." Jesus was there with them.

Floods and fires are good metaphors for abusive relationships. You may have felt swallowed up, scorched, or both. But the truth is that the Lord was there with you, you were never alone. And He will always be with you, no matter what.

She is Free Indeed

"Nebuchadnezzar responded and said, "Blessed be the God of Shadrach, Meshach and Abed-nego, who has sent His angel and delivered His servants who put their trust in Him, violating the king's command, and yielded up their bodies so as not to serve or worship any god except their own God."
Daniel 3:28 (NASB)

Reflection: Think of one of your most difficult times. Ask the Lord to show you where He was when it was happening.

Prayer: *Lord, thank You that You have never left me alone. Thank You that no matter where I am, no matter what I am going through, You are always there with me. I choose to put my trust completely in You.*

37

"Do not be afraid, for I am with you. I shall bring your offspring from the east, and gather you from the west. 6. To the north I shall say, 'Give them up!' and to the south, 'Do not hold them back!' Bring back my sons from far away, and my daughters from the remotest part of the earth, 7. everyone who bears my name, whom I have created for my glory, whom I have formed, whom I have made." Isaiah 43:5-7 (NJB)

The end of a relationship can be devastating for children no matter what their ages are. In some cases, the abuser has brainwashed the children into believing that their mother is crazy or that the failure of the relationship is her fault. Children sometimes turn their backs on their mothers and don't see or contact them for years. Others remain in relationship but struggle to trust. For a mother this is the worst kind of heartbreak.

It is important to know that God honors you as the mother of your children. His will is for them to be in a loving relationship with you. On this painful journey you need to keep holding onto faith that the Lord will restore those relationships. Pray for your children to see the truth about your situation. Know that your Heavenly Father's heart is hurting alongside yours. He above all, knows what it is like to have your children turn their backs on you. He so desperately wanted relationship with His children that He was willing to suffer and die a horrific death for it.

She is Free Indeed

When you pray to the Father about your children, His will and your will are in perfect harmony. He groans alongside you. Tears fall down His face as well.

"I have no greater joy than to hear that my children are walking in the truth." 3 John 1:4 (NIV)

Reflection: What action could you take today to give your fears about your children over to their Heavenly Father?

Prayer: *Lord you know my heart and you know how I long for my children to walk in truth. Please open their hearts and their eyes and their ears to see and hear and know the truth. Bring them into right relationship with both You and me.*

38

*"Yahweh says, 'You are my witnesses, my chosen servants.
I chose you in order that you would know me intimately,
believe me always, and fully understand that I am the only God.
There was no god before me,
and there will be no other god after me.'"*
Isaiah 43:10 (TPT)

What does it mean to know someone intimately? You attempted to have an intimate relationship with your former partner. It may indeed have even felt intimate for a while. But you were ultimately betrayed.

How does it feel to know that the Lord wants to know you intimately? Is it frightening? Daunting? Does it even feel possible? Perhaps you felt close to the Lord in the past but your toxic relationship got in the way.

You need to know that the Lord chose you. And He wants a close, intimate relationship with you. How do you know you can trust Him? Because He is the only God. There was no one before Him and there will never be another. He is trustworthy. He is faithful. He is the opposite of everything your partner was. Open your heart to Him. Let Him show you who He is. It doesn't mean that life will become easier. But it means you will have someone who is always by your side, always comforting and supporting you. Press in to know Him intimately. Ask Him to guide you as you read the Bible, as you worship and as you pray. His Holy Spirit is always right there-waiting for you to enter into conversation with Him.

"Trust in the Lord with all your heart
and lean not on your own understanding;
6 in all your ways submit to him,
and he will make your paths straight."
Proverbs 3:5-6 (NIV)

Reflection: What could you do today to increase your intimacy with the Lord?

Prayer: *Lord I want to know You more. Help me to know that I can trust You with everything. Thank You that You are always there. Help me to enter into true intimacy with You.*

39

I am God, yes, from eternity I am. No one can deliver from my hand; when I act, who can thwart me? 14. Thus says Yahweh, your redeemer, the Holy One of Israel: For your sake I have sent to Babylon, I shall knock down all the prison bars, and the Chaldaeans' shouts of joy will change to lamenta-tions. 15. I am Yahweh, your Holy One, the Creator of Israel, your king." Isaiah 43:13-15 (NJB)

The following are lyrics to the worship song, "The Lion and The Lamb,"[1]
Who can stop the Lord almighty?
Our God is the lion, the lion of Judah
He's roaring with power and fighting our battles
And every knee will bow before You

When He has purposed to act-no one can stop him. Sometimes we need to stop and remember just how powerful our God is. He is the creator of the universe. He holds time and eternity in his hands. He owns the keys to death and hell and he is the Most High. We see from these verses in Isaiah that his will is to break open prison doors and set prisoners free. Perfect and complete freedom won't come before Heaven, but the Lord still works to chip away at the things that bind us up. God is the Alpha and the Omega, the beginning and the end. He brought you to life and He will complete his work in you.

---

1. *Leeland Mooring / Brian Mark Johnson / Brenton Brown*

She is Free Indeed

You serve the King of kings and the Lord of lords. The Lion of the tribe of Judah is on your side. Who can stop you?

Then Jesus came to them and said, "All authority in Heaven and on earth has been given to me." Matthew 28:18 (NIV)

Reflection: Think about your future. Does the fact that nothing can stop God's ultimate will encourage you today?

Prayer: *I declare today that You are the Most High. I choose to put myself under Your authority and walk in all of Your ways.*

40

"No need to remember past events, no need to think about what was done before. 19.Look, I am doing something new, now it emerges; can you not see it? Yes, I am making a road in the desert and rivers in wastelands."
Isaiah 43:18-19 (TPT)

While it is impossible for us to forget the past, the Lord does not want us to wallow in it. While you are still suffering the effects of an abusive relationship, God wants you to know that there is healing and life ahead of you. He has something new for you.

References to the desert are common in the Bible. The Israelites wandered in the desert for 40 years, Elijah fled Jezebel through the desert. Jesus was tempted in the desert. The psalmists often refer to the desert. A common theme is that the Lord can and does miraculously bring rivers through the desert.

A river in the middle of the desert is impossible. But God does the impossible on a regular basis. While He created the laws of nature, He loves to play with them. He loves to surprise us. As you walk through this desert look for the rivers. God will bring them.

The road ahead of you will most likely be surprisingly different that you expect. Prepare yourself to be obedient to whatever the Lord is calling you to. Your experience does not disqualify you from anything in the Kingdom of God. In fact, God loves to use the broken and empty vessels for his glory.

"I will make rivers flow on barren heights, and springs within the valleys. I will turn the desert into pools of water, and the parched ground into springs."
Isaiah 41:18 (NIV)

Reflection: Think about your life. Where do you see little streams of water starting to flow?

Prayer: *Lord, help me to find You in the desert. Send me rivers of life. Help me to trust that You are always going to lead me.*

41

"Wild beasts, jackals, and owls will glorify me
For I supply streams of water in the desert
and rivers in the wilderness
to satisfy the thirst of my people, my chosen ones,
21 so that you, whom I have shaped and formed for myself,
will proclaim my praise."
Isaiah 43:20-21 (TPT)

We were created to glorify God. These verses speak of a time when the old has passed away, when all creation has been made new. This will happen at the end of earthly time. But from the beginning, the Lord wanted companionship. He wanted to have a love relationship with His children. When you were trapped in the prison of a destructive relationship, you were just trying to keep your head above the water. The idea of rivers in the desert, or animals peacefully praising the Lord was impossible for you to grasp. While you may have had a relationship with the Lord, it was challenging because your vision was so clouded.

Now that you are free, it's time to find hope in what is to come. It's also time to praise the Lord for all He has done and all He will do. As you get further and further away from that destructive relationship, you will be able to see more clearly where the Lord was and what He was doing during those awful times. Give Him glory. Praise Him for what He has done. And praise Him for what will be.

She is Free Indeed

"The wolf will live with the lamb, the leopard will lie down with the goat, the calf and the lion and the yearling together; and a little child will lead them." Isaiah 11:6 (NIV)

Reflection: Think about what the perfect relationship would look like for you. Then reflect on the fact that God is going to greatly surpass your expectations in your relationship with Him.

Prayer: *Thank you Lord for all You have done and all You will still do. Help me to hold on to the hope of what is to come. Let my life glorify You.*

42

"I am Yahweh, your Creator, who shaped you in my womb.
Hear what I have to say to you:
'Don't fear. I will help you, O Jacob my servant,
Do not fear, my pleasing one, Israel. I
will pour refreshing water on the thirsty
and streams on the dry ground."
Isaiah 44: 1b-3a (TPT)

Over and over again the Lord tells us not to fear. A destructive relationship chips away at your confidence and your sense of safety. Panic and anxiety attacks are a common and very normal part of recovery. But you need to know that all of those things your former partner said about you, and all of the things he is still saying about you are like words written in the sand. Instead of sitting there on that dry ground and allowing those words to bring you fear, Jesus wants to scoop you up, away from the sand and hold you in His arms. He then wipes away all of your tears in one stroke and sends the river in the desert that erases any sign of what was written there.

Your identity is found in Jesus, not in anything to do with your former partner. While there are no specific Biblical references to God as a mother, there are many metaphors that demonstrate his mother-heart. In this passage, he said, "I shaped you in my womb," (verse 1) If God acts as both mother and father, our complete genealogy is found in him.   Let Him comfort you in your fear today.

When I am afraid, I put my trust in you. Psalm 56:3 (NIV)

Reflection: How does the Lord demonstrate His mother heart?   What aspects of His character are mother-like?

Prayer: *Thank you Lord that you created me and you know me. Help me to remember to turn to You in my fear. Help me to learn how to rest in the peace of Your presence.*

43

"I will pour out my Spirit on your children,
my blessing upon your descendants.
4 They will spring up like grass blanketing a meadow,
like poplars growing by gushing streams. 5
One will say, "I belong to Yahweh."
Another will be called Jacob.
Yet another will write on his hand "Property of Yahweh."
Another will adopt the name Israel.""
Isaiah 44:3b-5 (TPT)

If you have children, they are probably heavy on your heart right now. They may have turned their backs on you. They may believe the story your former partner tells. And if they believe you, they are still mourning the end of what family used to be. While the above verses refer to the nation of Israel in the future, we can still use them to pray over our children. It is absolutely God's will for them to be in close relationship with Him. He is their true father and mother. They were His before they were yours. God also wants them to be in a healthy relationship with you, their mother.

While it is difficult to comprehend, it's important to remember that God is even more concerned for your children than you are. Remember that He shaped them in his own womb (Isaiah 44:1b). Hosea 2:14 (CJB) says, "But now I am going to woo her - I will bring her out to the desert and I will speak to her heart." Again, God is referring to the nation of Israel;

but these passages demonstrate the passion the Lord has for His children. Never give up praying for your children. Pray these passages over them. Know that the Lord has them constantly in mind.

"How often I have longed to gather your children together, as a hen gathers her chicks under her wings." Matthew 23:37b (NIV)

Reflection: Think about how much you love your children. Can you imagine how much the Father loves them?

Prayer: *Lord may my children know and proclaim You as God and father. May they know the truth so that they might be set free from the lies of the enemy. Get the obstacles out of the way that keep them from You. Help me to trust You with them.*

44

"Thus says Yahweh, Israel's king, Yahweh Sabaoth, his redeemer: I am the first and I am the last; there is no God except me. 7. Who is like me? Let him call out, let him affirm it and convince me it is so; let him say what has been happening since I instituted an eternal people, and predict to them what will happen next! 8. Have no fear, do not be afraid: have I not told you and revealed it long ago? You are my witnesses. Is there any God except me? There is no Rock; I know of none." Isaiah 44:6-8 (NJB)

It is time once again to reflect on the majesty of our God. He is the only God. He created this world and he will bring it to completion. He alone knows the future. He tells us yet again to not fear. Interestingly, there are 365 instances in the Bible where we are told not to fear. I doubt that that is a coincidence. There is a fear-not verse for every single day. I would suggest looking them up and printing them out and every day of the year, read at least one out loud. Claim your right to be free from fear.

God is the only rock. He is the only safe place. Your soul has never been at risk and it never will be. No matter what happens to you or around you, the Lord is there. It's an interesting juxtaposition that God is our rock, but also our place of warm and tender comfort. Hide behind that rock, rest in the everlasting arms. His Father heart is our strength and safety, his Mother heart is our peace, comfort and healing. Remember who your God is. Nothing can stop Him.

She is Free Indeed

"How great is our Lord! His power is absolute! His understanding is beyond comprehension!" Psalm 147:5 (NLT)

Reflection: What happens to your fears when you confront them with these Bible passages?

Prayer: *Thank you Lord for being my rock and my place of eternal safety. Teach me how to find shelter in You and comfort in Your arms. Help me to know that I need never fear the enemy.*

45

"I created you to be my servant, and I will never forget you!
22 I have swept away your sins like a thick cloud.
I have made your guilt to vanish
like mist disappearing into thin air.
Now come back, come back to me,
for I have paid the price for you."
Isaiah 44:21b-22 (TPT)

How often do we forget how big the grace of God is? How often do we bow our heads in shame and hesitate to enter His presence? The enemy loves to use our humanity against us. He loves to tell us that we are failures, that we aren't worthy of God's love, that our sin has caused a rift between us and our Father.

It's not true! The cross covered all sin, the sin of the past, present, and future. God is not surprised when we fail. He made provision for it. He never wants us to let shame keep us from His loving presence. When we sin, all we have to do is confess it and the Father picks us up, dusts us off, and puts us back on our feet again, and that's it! There's no penance, it's done. Psalm 103:12 (NIV) says, "As far as the east is from the west, so far has he removed our transgressions from us."

Come into your Father's presence with confidence today, knowing that you are clothed in the righteousness of Christ. Stop trying to be perfect in your own strength-it's simply not possible. Embrace His grace. It is there for you today.

"For our sake he made him to be sin who knew no sin, so that in him we might become the righteousness of God." 2 Corinthians 5:21 (ESV)

Reflection: Does guilt keep you from approaching the Lord? What does it mean to know that all of your sins have been completely forgiven?

Prayer: *Thank you, Lord that I can come boldly into Your presence, knowing I am always welcome. Guard my mind from the enemy's deception. May I always know how much I am loved.*

46

"Sing! Starry sky above, break loose with singing, for Yahweh has finished it!
Shout! Earth deep below, give up your shout!
Mountains high, break out with joyous songs of praise!
Let the forest choirs join in, with every tree singing its notes!
For Yahweh has paid the ransom price for Jacob's tribes,
and he will be glorified in Israel!" Isaiah 44:23 (TPT)

There are 3 foundations in our relationship with the Lord: prayer, praise and reading His word. Isa-iah keeps coming back to praise. In the middle of passages full of judgement there will be an interlude of praise. In the Psalms there are many times when, in the midst of agonizing complaints, the psalmist suddenly remembers the God he is writing about and interrupts those groans with praise for the Most High.

In the above passage Isaiah writes about how the beauty of creation praises the creator. When life is in shambles around you, the beauty of this world never fades. If you feel like you have nothing to praise the Lord for, look outside and join the mountains and trees and stars and sky in praise. Or pick up a leaf or flower and examine it closely. How intricately God has made each and every thing. And how much more precious to Him are you? And remember that your ransom has been paid. Jesus has set you free forever. As He said on the cross, "It is finished!" Your Father is right beside you. Your eternal home is secure. And as impossible as it may seem now, someday this will all pass away and you will remember it no more.

"The Heavens declare the glory of God; the skies proclaim the work of his hands." Psalm 19:1 (NIV)

Reflection: What are your favorite parts of nature? Think about how God's creation is another expression of His love for you.

Prayer: *Lord, help me to lift my vision from my problems today and to the beauty of Your creation. Help me to find things to praise You for when I am overwhelmed with sorrow.*

47

"Rain down, you Heavens, from above, and let the clouds pour down saving justice, let the earth open up and blossom with salvation, and let justice sprout with it; I, Yahweh, have created it!" Isaiah 45:8 (NJB)

Is God concerned with justice? Is He far off, just observing what is going on on the earth? Does He detach from what He is seeing? Absolutely not! God is the creator of justice. He himself is just. Deuteronomy 32:4 reads, "He is the Rock, his works are perfect, and all his ways are just. A faithful God who does no wrong, upright and just is he." Philip Yancey writes,

"I know of only one answer to the question, "Does God care?" and for me it has become decisive: Jesus is the answer. Jesus never attempted a philosophical answer to the problem of pain, yet he did give an existential answer. Although I cannot learn from him why a particular bad thing occurs, I can learn how God feels about it. Jesus gives God a face, and that face is streaked with tears."[1]

The Lord is longing for the day when He puts everything to right again. He longs to rain down His justice on behalf of the oppressed. I sometimes joke that God's favorite word is, "wait." But He always fulfills his promises. Keep holding on to faith and hope-justice for you is coming!

---

1. Yancey, Phillip. *The Bible Jesus Read.* Zondervan 2001

She is Free Indeed

"But let justice roll down like waters, and righteousness like an ever-flowing stream." Amos 5:24 (ESV)

Reflection: How would you answer the question, "Does God care?"

Prayer: *Thank you, Lord, that You embody justice. Thank You that You are concerned with my vindication. Thank you that justice is coming. Give me patience while I await it.*

48

"For thus says Yahweh, the Creator of the Heavens -- he is God, who shaped the earth and made it, who set it firm; he did not create it to be chaos, he formed it to be lived in: I am Yahweh, and there is no other. 19.I have not spoken in secret, in some dark corner of the underworld. I did not say, 'Offspring of Jacob, search for me in chaos!' I am Yahweh: I proclaim saving justice, I say what is true." Isaiah 45:18-19 (NJB)

God created a beautiful world for His children. His intent was that we would delight in Him and in His creation. He never intended for the world to descend into the chaos that we see in so many places today. Wars, sickness, lies, abuse-these were not a part of His plan. God is love, nothing born from hate comes from Him. God is light-in Him is no darkness at all. The idea that everything on earth happens because God allows it is a total contradiction to God's character. Why would God, allow the opposite of what He intended? Hate, fear, lies-none of these originate with God. The enemy brought those to this earth.

The Passion Translation of Isaiah 45:19b reads, "I didn't say to Jacob's tribes, 'Seek me in vain.'" If we keep our eyes fixed on what is going on in this earth it definitely feels like sometimes we seek the Lord in vain. But the Lord is very clear in the words that he spoke to Isaiah-seeking Him will never be in vain. The author of Ecclesiastes presents a negative view of life on earth. Ecclesiates 1:2-3 (NIV) reads,

She is Free Indeed

"Meaningless! Meaningless!"
   says the Teacher.
"Utterly meaningless!
   Everything is meaningless.
What do people gain from all their labors
   at which they toil under the sun?"

But this was written before Jesus had been sent to earth to restore our ability to have communion with the Lord. Lift your eyes today to the Heavens-seek that which nothing can take away from you.

1 John 4:19 (NIV) "We love because he first loved us."

Reflection: How does it feel to know that everything the Lord has ever said is true?

Prayer: *Thank you, Lord, for this beautiful world You made. Help me to remember to seek the things above and not the temporal things on this earth.*

49

"There is no other god except me, no saving God, no Saviour except me! 22.Turn to me and you will be saved, all you ends of the earth, for I am God, and there is no other. 23.By my own self I swear it; what comes from my mouth is saving justice, it is an irrevocable word: All shall bend the knee to me, by me every tongue shall swear, 24.saying, 'In Yahweh alone are saving justice and strength.'" Isaiah 45:21b-24a (NJB)

You may live in an area with good resources for women who have been abused. Or you may live where there is little help available to you. The question then becomes, "Where do I go for healing?" The verses above tell us that God alone has the power to save and to bring justice. Yes, you should avail yourself of any resources available to you, but if there is nothing, Jesus is enough. And even if there are lots of supports out there for you, you still need the original healer. 2 Corinthians 1:3 (NIV) "Praise be to the God and Father of our Lord Jesus Christ, the Father of compassion and the God of all comfort, who comforts us in all our troubles, so that we can comfort those in any trouble with the comfort we ourselves receive from God." If you are hurting, come before the Lord, enter His presence, reach out to Him with your hands, and let Him comfort you. It's easy to fall into despair thinking you will never be whole again. But as you continually come before the Lord and open your heart to His work, He will be faithful to complete it.

She is Free Indeed

"The righteous cry out, and the LORD hears them; he delivers them from all their troubles. 18 The LORD is close to the brokenhearted and saves those who are crushed in spirit," Psalm 37:17-22 (NIV)

Reflection: What does it mean to you to know that one of the ways God refers to Himself is as a healer?

Prayer: *I come to you, Yahweh Rapha, the Lord my healer. Please do Your deep work in my spirit. Help me to remember to keep coming to You first for my healing. Thank You for being so faithful.*

50

"Listen to me, O Jacob's tribes, all the remnant of Israel.
You never had to carry me, but I have carried you from birth.
I supported you from the moment you left the womb. 4 Even
as you grow old and your hair turns gray,
I'll keep carrying you!
I am your Maker and your Caregiver.
I will carry you and be your Savior."
Isaiah 46:3-4 (TPT)

Is it difficult for you to imagine that God has been with your since you were conceived? Do you worry that after this time of healing you might lose that intimacy you have with Him right now? Do you wonder if you can have the kind of intimacy you are searching for with Him? These verses are very clear. God was in it from the beginning and He will be in it until the end. You need never lose your intimacy with Him. There may be times of crisis when you feel His presence more and times when you might feel it less. He doesn't just swoop down in the critical times-He is there all of the time. It is interesting that these verses don't portray the Lord as leading or walking beside us-they demonstrate that He is actually carrying us. What a wonderful image that is.

God has an amazing way of taking the destruction that the enemy has wrought and creating something beautiful. Mosaics are beautiful pieces of art made from bits of shattered glass. While God did not will for you to experience trauma, if you let Him, He will gather up your broken pieces and create a masterpiece. Some day you will be able to look back on this time and say, "Look what the Lord has done."

"The LORD your God goes with you; he will never leave you nor forsake you." Deuteronomy 31:6b (NIV)

Reflection: Do you hide away the broken, hurting parts of your heart or do you let the Lord in to heal them?

Prayer: *Thank you, Lord, that You are always here and have always been here. Please take the broken pieces of my soul and create beauty from them.*

51

"Can't you see?
I have carved your name on the palms of my hands!
Your walls are always my concern."
Isaiah 49:16 (TPT)

Most translations use the word, "walls," in this passage, but the New Jerusalem Bible uses the word, "ramparts." While this verse is referring to the walls of Jerusalem, we can also apply it to our own lives. By definition, ramparts are defensive boundaries of fortified sites. Note the word, "boundaries." God encourages us to protect ourselves with boundaries. In your relationship many of your boundaries were completely disregarded, disrespected and were trampled over. An abusive man will not respect boundaries of any sort. You belonged to him and that was the end of the story.

So now, you gather up the broken pieces of your ramparts and try to reconstruct them. As an emotionally damaged person, you will need to make them bigger, you will need to push them further out than you have ever before. Many people will not understand these new boundaries of yours, but remember that they exist for your protection.

She is Free Indeed

Well known Christian psychologists write,

"Boundaries define us. They define what is me and what is not me. A boundary shows me where I end and someone else begins, leading me to a sense of ownership. Knowing what I am to own and take responsibility for gives me freedom. Taking responsibility for my life opens up many different options. Boundaries help us keep the good in and the bad out. Setting boundaries inevitably involves taking responsibility for your choices…you get what you tolerate." [1]

*"Above all else, guard your heart,
for everything you do flows from it."* Proverbs 4:23 (NIV)

Reflection: Think of a healthy boundary you could set for yourself today.

Prayer: *Father give me wisdom as I re-establish the boundaries You ordained for my protection. Help me to make them strong.*

---

1. Cloud, Henry, and Townsend, John. Boundaries. Zondervan. 1993

52

"But Yahweh says:
"The prey will be freed from the mighty warrior
and captives will be rescued from a conqueror!
For I will fight with those who fight with you,
and I myself will save your children."
Isaiah 49:25 (TPT)

Do you feel alone in this battle? Do you feel as though you will never regain that which you have lost? Does the Lord feel far off? Daniel, prophet in the Old Testament, once had a vision that deeply disturbed him. He spent 3 weeks praying and fasting, waiting to hear from the Lord. When the angel God sent finally came, he said, "Don't be afraid, Daniel. God has heard everything that you said ever since the first day you decided to humble yourself in front of your God so that you could learn to understand things. I have come in response to your prayer." Daniel 10:12 (GWT) All that time, the Lord was working even though Daniel couldn't see it or feel it. The angel goes on to tell Daniel that there was a battle he had to fight before he could deliver his message. God wasn't just sitting back and making Daniel wait-He was working! He was fighting! There may be months that go by before you see solutions to your problems. It may feel as though there are no answers sometimes. When you don't see it, when you don't feel it, put your name in this verse, instead of Daniel's, and know deep within your heart that God is still working.

She is Free Indeed

"Clearly, you are a God who works behind the scenes, God of Israel, Savior God." Isaiah 45:15 (MSG)

Reflection: Looking back on all you have been through; can you now see where the Lord was working alongside you?

Prayer: *Thank you Lord that You are always working. When I feel despair, help me to remember all of the things You have already done so that I can have faith to know You will keep on working on my behalf.*

53

"Morning by morning, he awakens my heart.
He opens my ears to hear his voice, to be trained to teach.
The Lord Yahweh has opened my ear,
and I did not resist; I did not rebel."
Isaiah 50:4b-5 (TPT)

This passage is a Messianic song-it refers to the coming Jesus. But we can apply these words to ourselves as well. The Lord longs to speak to our open ears, to our open hearts. He longs to teach us. It is so easy to become distracted by our own needs, the pain of those we love, and the busyness of our post-modern lifestyles. Do you take time at some point during the day to settle your soul at the feet of your Father to listen to what He has to say to you? I think sometimes we avoid listening to His voice out of fear of what we think He might say. We wait for a slap on the wrist, thinking we are condemned. But He is always gentle and loving and encouraging.

If you have children, think of their sweet little faces first thing in the morning. No matter how tired you are, you delight to see them (well, most days!). That is how our Father feels about us. You never need to fear His presence. Think of the people who dragged their sin-steeped souls to Jesus in the scriptures. Which one who came in humility did He ever condemn? No one. So come. Sit at His feet so that he can pour out His love on you.

She is Free Indeed

"Let him lead me to the banquet hall, and let his banner over me be love."
Song of Solomon 2:4 (NIV)

Reflection: What holds you back from opening yourself completely to the Lord?

Prayer: *Lord help me to enter Your presence with my head held high, knowing that I come to You as Your beloved daughter. Teach me to listen so that I can hear Your words of life for me.*

54

"He who grants me saving justice is near! Who will bring a case against me? Let us appear in court together! Who has a case against me? Let him approach me! 9.Look, Lord Yahweh is coming to my help! Who dares con-demn me? Look at them, all falling apart like moth-eaten clothes! 10.Which of you fears Yahweh and listens to his servant's voice? Which of you walks in darkness and sees no light? Let him trust in the name of Yahweh and lean on his God!"
Isaiah 50:8-10 (NJB)

What a beautiful picture of what is to come. While the Lord will certainly fight for you in the earthly courts, He does not control the minds of judges and lawyers any more than He does anyone else. Your experiences in court may be good ones, or they may be horrible ones. But take heart! These verses promise that at the end of time, no one will be able to condemn you-not your former partner, no lawyers, no judges, no family members and no pastors. God will be the judge and jury and He has already acquitted you. On that day everyone will watch as you enter into His glory with a gorgeous crown on your head and clothed in the white robes of Christ, which are brighter than the sun. The last words of this passage are beautiful. Are you leaning on your God? Are you letting Him carry you or are you rushing ahead trying to make things work out on your own? It's never too late to stop, to breathe and remember Who it is who is fighting for you. Picture yourself curled up in his lap today. If you can't handle seeing your future on this earth right now, look to the future in Heaven that He has promised you.

"For the Lord is our judge; the Lord is our lawgiver; the Lord is our king; he will save us." Isaiah 33:22 (ESV)

Reflection: What is an area of your life that you could let go of trying to fix on your own and lean on the Lord for help with?

Prayer: *Thank you Lord, that my future is in Your hands and that it is nothing but light and love. Help me to lift my weary head to look to You. Teach me to lean on You at all times.*

55

"Listen to me, you who chase after righteousness,
you who passionately pursue the Lord.
Look back to Abraham, the rock from which you were cut,
to Sarah, the quarry from which you were dug,
and remember what I did for them.
Yes, look to Abraham your father and to Sarah, who bore you.
For when I called Abraham, he was but one person,
but I blessed him greatly so that one became many."
Isaiah 51:1-2 (TPT)

As Christians we have the incredible blessing of being able to read the Bible which tells the story from the beginning of time to the story of the first churches. We are able to read about the journeys of so many men and women who sought the Lord. As you read, you will notice that there is not a single easy story in the Bible. No one had a path paved with gold. Everyone struggled. But we are able to look back on those stories and see the faithfulness of God. Some Bible characters, such as Abraham and Joseph waited many many years for the promises of God to be fulfilled in their lives. Some characters, like Moses and David, stumbled and fell over and over and over again. But no matter what their lives looked like; God kept His promises to them. His promises were not dependent on how faithful to him they were themselves.

When you feel frustrated with the waiting, when you begin to feel despair, open up your Bible and start to read. You will find story after story where God came through for His children. He never failed. Not once. And he will never fail you.

"Not one word of all the good promises that the LORD had made to the house of Israel had failed; all came to pass." Joshua 21:45 (ESV

Reflection: Think of your favorite Bible characters. How do their stories encourage you today?

Prayer: *Lord, help me to hold on to You when I feel discouraged. Help me to remember that You never fail and that You will always be faithful to me.*

56

"Indeed, Yahweh will comfort Zion, restore her,
and comfort all her broken places.
He will transform her wilderness into the garden of Bliss,
her desert into the garden of Yahweh.
Joy and laughter will fill the air
with thanksgiving and joyous melodies."
Isaiah 51:3 (TPT)

In the last devotional we talked about God's faithfulness to fulfill His promises. Today as the passage goes on, we see the things He has promised. The first is comfort. When children are small, if they fall and get hurt, they come running to their parents, with tear streaked faces and arms lifted high to be picked up. A loving parent scoops that little one up and holds the child close and comforts him or her. That is exactly how we need to come to Jesus when we are hurting.

Next, He promises to restore. You have lost so many things-possibly your finances, your reputation, family and friends. Know that the Father is actively working to restore those things to you, but also remember that restoration cannot be completed here on earth. Keep your eyes on the things to come.

Then He refers to our broken places. Kintsugi is the Japanese art of mending broken pottery with lacquer that has gold in it. These become absolutely beautiful pieces of art. That is what God wants to do with your broken pieces.

Further on He talks about transforming our wilderness and deserts into a garden. The Hebrew word here is the word for "Eden." Eden was paradise.

Finally, this verse mentions laughter, joy, thanksgiving and music. Doesn't that seem like the opposite of what you feel right now? Take heart. Your Eden is coming.

"Let us hold unswervingly to the hope we profess, for he who promised is faithful." Hebrews 10:23 (NIV)

Reflection: Which of these promises encourage you the most? How can you hold onto them today?

Prayer: *Lord help me to remember to come to You first with my pain. Let me feel Your comfort today. Give me hope for my future.*

57

"So listen to me, you who know what saving justice means, a people who take my laws to heart: do not fear people's taunts, do not be alarmed by their insults, 8.for the moth will eat them like clothing, the grub will devour them like wool, but my saving justice will last for ever and my salvation for all generations." Isaiah 51:7-8 (TPT)

You have likely been the recipient of many harsh and negative words. You have surely faced insults on a variety of levels. Yet these verses tell us basically to completely disregard those insults. That's easier said than done. Back in Isaiah 37 Sennacherib, ruler of Assyria, had sent threats to Hezekiah king of Judah. When his ministers consulted the prophet Isaiah, he assured them that there was nothing to worry about. But again, Sennacherib sent more threats-mocking God and His ability to help Judah. This second time, Hezekiah took the letter from his enemy into the Temple of the Lord. He spread it out before the Lord and again asked for wisdom. God again sent word through Isaiah that Judah had nothing to fear.

When you receive hurtful and insulting messages, when you receive threatening legal documents, don't let yourself immediately despair. Take those words and spread them out before the Lord. Ask Him to remind you of His promises, ask Him to give you peace instead of fear. Ask Him to take away the power those words have over you. Say out loud, "I will not fear the words of my enemies. My God's saving justice will last forever!"

The Lord will vindicate me;
your love, Lord, endures forever —
do not abandon the works of your hands.
Psalm 138:8 (NIV)

Reflection: What accusation or lie is heaviest on your heart today? How can you release it to the Lord?

> **Prayer:** *Lord break the power of these negative words over me. Help me to remember that You are the only one with real authority in my life!*

58

*"Wasn't it you who dried up the Red Sea with its deep waters
and made a path through the sea to rescue your redeemed?
Do it again! Those Yahweh has set free
will return to Zion and come celebrating with songs of joy!
They will be crowned with never-ending joy!
Gladness and joy will overwhelm them;
despair and depression will disappear!"
Isaiah 51:10-11 (TPT)*

When God parted the waters of the Red Sea so that the Israelites could escape Egypt, what was His intention? Did He lead them out just to let them starve in the wilderness? No, that was not His plan. And when God led you out of your Egypt did He let you drown in the Red Sea or starve in the wilderness? No. "Returning to Zion," is about coming home. While you may still be in your physical home, the Lord wants to invite you into your spiritual home-close relationship with Him. Right now, we live in the already-not yet stage of the Kingdom of God. We get to experience glimpses of Heaven. In that place of intimacy with God we can celebrate and be crowned with never-ending joy. We can sing and dance as we unite our souls with our Saviour and Creator. Can you imagine being overwhelmed with gladness and joy? It's difficult to believe that it is possible, but it is! When we enter the true home of our souls, despair and depression disappear. Let these moments of bliss give you hope for your future. You have not reached your final home yet. But glimpses of His glory can sustain you as you wait.

"But as it is written:
"What eye has not seen, and ear has not heard,
and what has not entered the human heart,
what God has prepared for those who love him,"
1 Corinthians 2:9 (NASB)

Reflection: What is holding you back from joy today? How could you release it to the Lord?

Prayer: *Thank You Jesus, for leading me out of Egypt. Thank You that the Promised Land lies ahead of me. Help me to daily enter Your presence to get that glimpse of eternity and help me hold on to hope.*

59

"I, yes I, am the one who comforts you.
All the sons of men will be cut down and fade like grass.
Why then would you be afraid of a mere human being?
You have forgotten that Yahweh, your Maker,
stretched out the skies and laid earth's firm foundation.
But you live each day constantly worrying,
living in fear of your angry oppressor
who is bent on your destruction.
But their fury cannot touch you! Those who are suffering will soon be released.
They will not die in their dark dungeon,
nor will they go hungry.
For I am Yahweh, your faithful God,
who split the sea with its roaring waves.
My name is Lord Yahweh, Commander of Angel Armies!"
Isaiah 51:12-15 (TPT)

These are strong words reminding us again of the ultimate power of
 the God we serve. There is none
who can match His might. In Isaiah, God instructs us again and again to not fear our oppressors. It is so difficult not to fall into that pattern of constant worry. Your former partner and his threats and accusations may weigh heavily upon you. How do those words, "But their fury cannot touch you," make you feel? Does it give you hope or do you still feel overwhelmed? Having been so close to someone for so long, it is very hard to extricate your emotions from that destructive relationship. I would encourage you to read these verses aloud, to declare that your God is the one who can split the sea. Remember that He is

the Commander of Angel Armies. No one can stop Him. And yet, while filled with power and might, He is also the God who wants to hold you and speak tenderly to you. He wants to be your true husband. The One who protects you by His might and comforts you with His love.

"Have I not commanded you? Be strong and courageous. Do not be afraid; do not be discouraged, for the LORD your God will be with you wherever you go." Joshua 1:9 (NIV)

Reflection: How would your life be different if you consistently held on to the truth of Joshua 1:9?

Prayer: *Thank You Lord that You are all-powerful. Help me to remember to come to You first when I am afraid. Help me to trust in Your protection.*

60

"Wake up! Open your eyes!
Beautiful Zion, put on your majestic strength!
Jerusalem, the sacred city,
put on your glory garments!
Never again will the unclean enter your gates! Arise and shake off your dust!
Sit enthroned, Jerusalem!
Break off your shackles of bondage from your neck,
you captive daughter of Zion!"
Isaiah 52:1-2 (TPT)

These verses refer to the captivity of the nations of Israel and Judah. God was promising them that they would one day be free. When the Lord showed you that you were in an abusive relationship, He woke you up. It is interesting that the first instruction after, "wake up!" is to put on your beautiful garments. What are those garments? They are the glorious robes of the righteousness of Christ. There is no shame attached to you. You are completely and totally redeemed. The next instruction is to stand up and shake off the dust you were covered with during your relationship. As you stand and brush away that debris, you may find yourself unrecognizable-there you are-a beautiful woman once more. "Break off your shackles of bondage from your neck, you captive daughter of Zion." What profound words. It is interesting that he didn't say, "I will break off your shackles." It seems as if it is in our own power to break them off. It's like God opens the door to your prison,

She is Free Indeed

but then you have to actually step out of it. Now that you are awake, clothed in righteousness, untarnished, unstained, beautiful and free-walk in it. Hold your head high. You are the redeemed of the Lord!

"Therefore the redeemed of the LORD shall return, and come with singing unto Zion; and everlasting joy shall be upon their head: they shall obtain gladness and joy; and sorrow and mourning shall flee away."
Isaiah 51:11 (KJV)

Reflection: Are there things in your life that are still holding you in chains today? Can you trust the Lord to break those chains?

Prayer: *Lord help me to embrace the fullness of my freedom. Thank You for waking me up and enabling me to walk free from my former prison. Help me to hold on to the truth of who I am in You.*

61

"Therefore, my people will know the power of my name,
and they will know in that day
that I am the one who promised them, saying,
'Behold, I am here!'
What a beautiful sight to behold—
the precious feet of the messenger
coming over the mountains to announce good news!
He comes to refresh us with wonderful news,
announcing salvation to Zion and saying,
"Your Mighty God reigns!"
Isaiah 52:6-7 (TPT)

Do you know the power of His name? Do you know that He is here? Do you know that he reigns?

When you are afraid, He says, "I am here!" When you are exhausted, He says, "know the power of my name!" When the future seems daunting, He says, "Your mighty God reigns!" When everything around you is dark and foreboding, He says, "I have wonderful news!" When the darkness tries to pull you under, He says, "I have announced your salvation!"

How lovely are the feet of He who has brought about your freedom! Luke 7:37-38 describes a woman who was a, "sinner," coming to the home of a Pharisee where Jesus was eating with His disciples. She fell at His feet and wept and washed them with her tears, then wiped them with her hair and finally rubbed them with perfume. The cultural significance of this act was profound, but we can look at it simply as an invitation: He calls us to come to His feet, sit there and cry our tears and now He is the one who pours out the oil of joy upon us in exchange for our tears.

"For this reason I say to you, her sins, which are many, have been forgiven, for she loved much; but he who is forgiven little, loves little."
Luke 7:47 (NASB)

Reflection: What are some of the things that remind you of the greatness of God?

Prayer: *Jesus, help me to remember the peace and the joy and the love that can be found by simply sitting at Your feet, in Your presence. Speak to me as I open up my heart to listen.*

> *"Go! Go, and leave Babylon behind!*
> *Touch nothing unclean as you depart.*
> *Keep your life pure as you leave,*
> *you who carry the vessels of Yahweh!*
> *You will neither have to leave in haste,*
> *nor will you make a frantic escape,*
> *for your God, Yahweh, will go before you.*
> *He will lead you each step and be your rear guard."*
> Isaiah 52:11-12 (TPT)

The Israelites spent around 70 years in captivity in Babylon. Your captivity was likely not that long, but it probably felt like hundreds of years. Now that you are free, it is sometimes tempting to look back, to wonder if you should have left. Your life might be in upheaval, you may feel unbalanced and sometimes what is familiar can seem safer even when it is not. But the Lord does not want you to go back to your captivity.

It also might be tempting to try to jump into a new relationship. It's hard to feel whole alone. But it is critically important that you don't. You need to follow after Yahweh who goes before you and behind you. You have healing to do. You have wholeness to find that can only be found in a relationship with Jesus. It is hard. It will likely be the loneliest time you have experienced in your life. But it is also the time when you will walk the most closely with your Lord. You will learn to lean on him, to trust Him for every

She is Free Indeed

breath, to go to Him first for comfort. It doesn't come naturally-you must cultivate it. But it will be eternally worth it.

"The eternal God is your refuge, and underneath are the everlasting arms."
Deuteronomy 33:27a (NIV)

Reflection: What are some specific ways you can rely upon the Lord today?

Prayer: *Lord, go before me and behind me. Help me to run to You first and find my identity in You alone. Help me to remember that You are my source.*

63

"He had no form or charm to attract us, no beauty to win our hearts; 3. he was despised, the lowest of men, a man of sorrows, familiar with suffering, one from whom, as it were, we averted our gaze, despised, for whom we had no regard. 4. Yet ours were the sufferings he was bearing, ours the sorrows he was carrying, while we thought of him as someone being punished and struck with affliction by God;" Isaiah 53:2b-4 (NJB)

Isaiah 53 is a prophecy relating to the coming Messiah. It is not a pretty picture which is why so many Jews, both in times past and present have rejected Jesus. These verses portray the Messiah as uncompromisingly human. There is no suffering common to humankind that Jesus himself did not experience. Have you felt less than beautiful? So did He. Have you been despised? So has He. Do judgmental people look down on you? They did so to Him as well. Do people you used to know and love turn away if they see you? They did that to Him, too. Are your words disregarded? So were His. Have you lost the regard of those you respected? So did He. He bore your suffering, He carried your sorrows, He was punished and struck with affliction for you. Our Savior is not sitting back in heaven distantly peering down at us. He has walked the road of humanity Himself. He has experienced everything you have experienced.

So where can you go to be understood? You can go to Jesus. Where can you go for empathy? You can go to Jesus. Where can you go to find your worth? You can go to Jesus.

"Come to me, all you who are weary and burdened, and I will give you rest." Matthew 11:28 (NIV)

Reflection: What is something from your past that you could bring before the Lord today to ask Him for His healing?

Prayer: *Thank You Lord, that You are intimately acquainted with all of my sorrows. You understand my pain. Thank You that You can relate to me completely. May my eyes always see You clearly.*

64

"Rejoice with singing, you barren one!
You who have never given birth,
burst into a song of joy and shout,
you who have never been in labor!
For the deserted wife will have more children
than the married one," says Yahweh.
"Increase is coming, so enlarge your tent
and add extensions to your dwelling.
Hold nothing back! Make the tent ropes longer and the pegs stronger.
You will increase and spread out in every direction.
Your sons and daughters will conquer nations
and revitalize desolate cities."
Isaiah 54:1-3 (TPT)

These verses refer to Israel's return from captivity. They portray the opposite of the captivity experience. How does one who has been barren, "rejoice with singing…burst into a song of joy and shout?" This is a metaphor for the desolate. The coming freedom and salvation are worth much more than having figuratively born children. It can be compared to having many children who will, "conquer nations." When God says, "hold nothing back!" He is saying that the joy that is to come will be way beyond your imagination. Don't let your imagination limit what God can do.

This all means that your life is going to be fruitful. Your time has not passed, it is now. Nothing can limit what God can do in and through you. He is ready to

She is Free Indeed

begin. Are you? Are you open to new things? Are you willing to take risks? Your life is probably going to be drastically different than you ever imagined. And that's a good thing because God has a much better imagination than you do! Nothing in your past limits what God can do with your future. Be alert-watch for the opportunities He is going to bring you.

"Brothers and sisters, I do not consider myself yet to have taken hold of. But one thing I do: Forgetting what is behind and straining toward what is ahead, 14 I press on toward the goal to win the prize for which God has called me heavenward in Christ Jesus." Philippians 3:13-14 (NIV)

Reflection: Think of an opportunity the Lord has opened up for you lately. Are you on board?

Prayer: *Thank You, Lord for what You are going to do through me. Help me to be open and ready when You want to move in me.*

65

"Do not fear, for your shame is no more.
Do not be embarrassed,
for you will not be disgraced.
You will forget the inadequacy you felt in your youth
and will no longer remember the shame of your widowhood.
For your Maker is your husband;
his name is Yahweh, Commander of Angel Armies!
Your Kinsman-Redeemer is the Holy One of Israel!
He has the title Mighty God of All the Earth!"
Isaiah 54:4-5 (TPT)

Here again we have the command, "Do not fear!" But this one is in regard to your shame. Some cultures assign shame to widows, even to the point of killing them. While you may not have been literally widowed, having a partner no longer can elicit the same shame. But God has promised that your shame is, "no more!" He has taken the role of your husband and He is the commander of angel armies. He is the mightiest of mighty ones. No one can take you from His hand. He does not want you to be embarrassed, He wants you to walk with your head held high like the daughter of a king you are! Disgrace refers to a loss of respect, honor and esteem. God is saying that you are worthy of respect, you are honored and He holds you in high esteem. How highly must He view you if he calls you His bride?

It is time to leave the fear, shame, inadequacy, disgrace and embarrassment behind. Take hold of the hand of your God and walk in His grace. Let your face shine with His light-He has chosen you and accepted you for who you are. He delights in you!

"For the Lord takes delight in his people; he crowns the humble with victory." Psalm 149:4 (NIV)

Reflection: Is there a failure or some shame in your past that you need to be freed from? Bring it before the Lord today so that he can wash it all away.

Prayer: *Thank You, Jesus, that when I take Your hand, I leave all of the past behind. Thank You that You have redeemed me. Help me to walk in a constant awareness of Your grace.*

66

"Should anyone attack you, that will not be my doing, and whoever does attack you, for your sake will fall...No weapon forged against you will suc-ceed. Any voice raised against you in court you will refute. Such is the lot o f the servants of Yahweh, the saving justice I assure them, declares Yahweh."
Isaiah 54:15, 17 (NJB)

In these verses, God is assuring us that when people rise up against you to attack you-that does not come from Him. Those attacks are not His will or in His plans for you. In fact, He promises that anyone who tries to attack you will ultimately fail. Weapons formed against you will prove futile in the end. Any false word spoken against you in court will be struck down. God assures you of His saving justice. In the end you will rise and those who have tried to tear you down will fall.

In the meantime, it is understandably difficult to maintain hope. It is hard to wait. But it is so important that you remind yourself of these words over and over and over again. Hold fast to the knowledge that your vindication is coming. The deeds of darkness will be exposed. The ultimate Judge has assured us that He will deliver His saving justice for his servants. God wants to heal the wounds of your soul from the attacks you have received. He hates those attacks even more than you do. He is going to redeem them. He is going to heal you. He will restore you to a place of honor. When the day comes that every knee shall

She is Free Indeed

bow before Him-you will be counted among the righteous.

"For he has set a day when he will judge the world with justice by the man he has appointed." Acts 17:31a (NIV)

Reflection: Imagine that day, when the whole world will know the truth. How will you feel when that happens?

Prayer: *Thank You Lord, that You are the ultimate judge and You will give me the justice that I long for. Give me patience and hope while I wait for it.*

67

"Oh, come to the water all you who are thirsty; though you have no money, come! Buy and eat; come, buy wine and milk without money, free! 2. Why spend money on what cannot nourish and your wages on what fails to satis-fy? Listen carefully to me, and you will have good things to eat and rich food to enjoy. 3. Pay attention, come to me; listen, and you will live. I shall make an everlasting covenant with you." Isaiah 55:1-3a (NJB)

The Lord delights in His children. He longs for relationship with us. He knows that He alone can meet our needs. How often we turn to other things to meet our hunger and thirst. We forget that the Most High has a river of living water flowing from His throne. We forget that if we partake of Him, we will never hunger or thirst again. He says, "Listen, and you will live." What do we listen to? We listen to His word which gives life, and we listen to His Holy Spirit who breathes on our souls.

I once said to the Lord that I felt guilty for my many blessings. I told him that He should send them instead to someone like an HIV+ woman in Africa, living in abject poverty, raising children on her own, knowing she will leave them orphaned some day. He told me, "That woman is far richer than you. You have everything-she has to trust me for every single mouthful of food she feeds her children, for every minute that she is alive. She is rich in her relationship with Me."

She is Free Indeed

All things can be found in Him. If we are willing to trust, and throw ourselves on His mercy He will meet all of our needs.

"And my God will meet all your needs according to the riches of his glory in Christ Jesus." Philippians 4:19 (NIV)

Reflection: What is a worry you have been struggling with. Do you believe that God is going to provide?

Prayer: *Thank You lord for the sustenance You provide. Help me to come every day, to eat and drink at Your table.*

68

"Seek the Lord Yahweh when he makes himself approachable
call upon him when you sense he is near.
The wicked need to abandon their ways,
and sinful ones need to banish every evil thought.
Let them return to Yahweh,
and they will experience his compassionate mercy.
Yes, let them return to God,
for he will lavish forgiveness upon them."
Isaiah 55:6-7 (TPT)

As you work on your own healing, you want to put your former partner out of your mind as much as possible. However, it is good to remember that he is still a child of God in need of His love and acceptance. Abusers tend to suffer from a lot of shame and they often see God as harsh and distant. The Lord longs for them to come into relationship with Him. Their hardness of heart breaks God's heart.

"I shall pour clean water over you and you will be cleansed; I shall cleanse you of all your filth and of all your foul idols. 26.I shall give you a new heart, and put a new spirit in you; I shall remove the heart of stone from your bodies and give you a heart of flesh instead. 27.I shall put my spirit in you, and make you keep my laws, and respect and practise my judgements."
Ezekiel 36:25-27 (NJB)

She is Free Indeed

Reflection: Are you ready to pray for your former partner? It's ok if you don't feel ready. Try just reading the following prayer aloud.

> **Prayer:** *Lord I bring _____ before you. I pray that he would be prompted to seek You. I pray that he would understand that he can call on You and that You will be there for him. I pray that You would help him to leave behind his destructive behaviours and that You would help him to put the past behind him. I pray that You would open his eyes to see the remarkable love You have for him. May You take away his heart of stone and give him a new heart. I pray that You would lead him into your presence so that he can experience Your compassionate mercy. May he return to you to so that he can embrace Your forgiveness and be healed. I pray that he will trust You with his pain and know you as the loving, gentle Father that you are. Lord I ask that _____ would be radically saved. I pray that You would put your Spirit in him so that he will be transformed and will walk in Your light. Bring him to a place of complete healing.*

69

"For, as the rain and the snow come down from the sky and do not return before having watered the earth, fertilising it and making it germinate to provide seed for the sower and food to eat, 11.so it is with the word that goes from my mouth: it will not return to me unfulfilled or before having carried out my good pleasure and having achieved what it was sent to do."
Isaiah 55:10-11 (NJB)

The New Jerusalem Bible includes a note on these verses, "The word of Yahweh is like a messenger who does not return until he has discharged his mission." There are so many times where we feel as though we are left in the dark, waiting for an answer. But God is working. He is always working. And He will keep working until all of His promises are fulfilled. CH Spurgeon writes,

"The Lord, when he hath given great faith, has been known to try it by long delays...But we must be careful not to take delays in prayer for denials: God's long-dated bills will be punctually honoured; we must not suffer Satan to shake our confidence in the God of truth by pointing to our unanswered prayers. Unanswered petitions are not unheard. God keeps a file for our prayers--they are not blown away by the wind, they are treasured in the King's archives. This is a registry in the court of heaven wherein every prayer is recorded."[1]

---

1. *Morning and Evening.* Hendrickson Publishers. 1997

She is Free Indeed

When all you hear is silence, when it seems like everything has stalled, remember that God is on the way. He does so many things behind the scenes that we will never know about while we are on this earth. While you may think He is ignoring you, remember that He is that messenger who is intent on carrying out His mission. Your God is coming.

"This is the confidence we have in approaching God: that if we ask anything according to his will, he hears us. And if we know that he hears us—whatever we ask—we know that we have what we asked of him." 1 John 5:14-15 (NIV)

Reflection: Think about a time when God showed his faithfulness to you. Thank Him for what He did.

Prayer: *Lord, help me to remember that you are always working on my behalf. In the dark, quiet times, strengthen my faith. Guard my heart from the enemy's lies. Thank You that You have always been faithful and that You will always be faithful.*

70

"For you will leave your exile with joy
and be led home wrapped in peace.
The mountains and hills in front of you will burst into singing and the trees of
the field will applaud! Cypress trees will flourish where there were only thorns
and myrtle trees instead of nettles.
These will stand as a testimony to Yahweh's renown,
everlasting signs that will not be cut off."
Isaiah 55:12-13 (TPT)

These verses are such a beautiful promise of what
is to come. As you began this walk, leaving your partner behind you, the journey described in these verses began. You may not yet feel joy, or the experience of it may be fleeting. But total and complete joy has been promised to you. And can you imagine being wrapped in peace? There will be many moments when that sounds absurd, and you wonder how you can have peace in the midst of these circumstances. But you can and you will. It will feel like you have a thick, warm blanket wrapped around you. Beautiful things will begin to grow in you where previously there were weeds and thistles. The images of creation rejoicing in these verses represent the joy the Lord feels when His children are walking with Him. The Lord did indeed rejoice when you left your abusive relationship. He wants his daughters to be free. While we will not experience the fullness of this on earth, we can fix our eyes on Jesus, knowing that complete joy, complete peace, and complete safety are only found

She is Free Indeed

in Him. And we will experience the fullness of these when we arrive at our true home, Heaven, where we will be with Him forever.

"You will keep in perfect peace all who trust in you, all whose thoughts are fixed on you!" Isaiah 26:3 (NLT)

Reflection: Sit before the Lord today and ask Him to show You what His perfect peace feels like.

Prayer: *Thank You, Jesus, that in You I can find perfect peace. Thank You for the joy You promise. Help me to find them in You as I come before You today.*

71

"For this is what the high and majestic one says,
the one who fills the eternal realm with glory, whose name is Holy:
"I dwell in high and holy places
but also with the bruised and lowly in spirit,
those who are humble and quick to repent.
I dwell with them to revive the spirit of the humble,
to revive the heart of those who are broken over their sin.
You will not find me continually accusing them
or holding anger against them, lest they feel defeated and lose heart before me.
For I am the One who gave the breath of life to my people."
Isaiah 57:15-16 (TPT)

These verses are a beautiful depiction of the way the Almighty, Creator of Heaven and earth, the Most Holy One, lowers Himself to comfort the afflicted. Rarely will we see a billionaire beside a homeless person. They might throw money to a charity, but to get personally involved would seem distasteful. And yet who does the King of kings and the Lord of lords associate with? He communes with the bruised and the broken, the humble and the hurting. God does not come to us with a list of things He wants us to change. He comes to us breathing life into our spirits. He comes to strengthen our hearts. He has nothing but compassion for our weary souls.

Hebrews 4:16 (NIV) says, "Let us then approach God's throne of grace with confidence, so that we may receive mercy and find grace to help us in our time of need." The throne of God is, "the throne of grace." Grace is the opposite of judgement. No one need ever approach that throne with shame. No judgement will be found there. Don't let the enemy fool you back into feeling shame and self-doubt. Don't let him lie to you that you are to blame. When you remember those words your partner used against you, reject them in Jesus' name. Jesus has given you the authority to do that. So approach His throne of grace with your head held high in the confidence that you are wrapped up in His righteousness.

"God made him who had no sin to be sin for us, so that in him we might become the righteousness of God." 2 Corinthians 5:21 (NIV)

Reflection: Is there something in your life that you haven't forgiven yourself for? Do you know that the Lord has completely forgiven you for it?

Prayer: *Lord help me to come to Your throne room of grace with confidence. Meet me there so that You can breathe life and healing back into my soul. Guard my mind from the enemy's lies. Thank You that You are gentle and filled with compassion.*

72

"Is not this the kind of fasting I have chosen:
to loose the chains of injustice
and untie the cords of the yoke,
to set the oppressed free
and break every yoke?
Is it not to share your food with the hungry
and to provide the poor wanderer with shelter—
when you see the naked, to clothe them,
and not to turn away from your own flesh and blood?
Then your light will break forth like the dawn,
and your healing will quickly appear;
then your righteousness[will go before you,
and the glory of the Lord will be your rear guard.
Then you will call, and the Lord will answer;
you will cry for help, and he will say: Here am I."
Isaiah 58:6-9a (NIV)

There are almost 80 references to fasting in the Bible. It was almost considered a sacrament in biblical times. In these verses, the Lord is saying that when we want to see true deliverance, freedom and healing, fasting is one of the ways we can achieve them. In fasting, we humble ourselves to the place of denying a need. In the type of fast mentioned above, it also involves being generous to those who are needy. In this twofold fast we are promised great things. We are promised that the Lord will hear our prayers. We are promised deliverance.

Not everyone has the health to support food fasts. Food fasts can also be done in ways such as the Daniel fast where your body is getting nutritional support while denying yourself things you crave. If food fasting is not an option for you, I would encourage you to pray and ask the Lord what he wants you to fast. It could be technology, TV, sugar, coffee, fast food, social media, etc. The point is to deny yourself. And when you do, the Lord promises to meet you there and work His miraculous power.

"Even now," declares the LORD, "return to me with all your heart, with fasting and weeping and mourning." Joel 2:12 (NIV)

Reflection: What is something in your life that is taking too much of your time? What would giving it up for a time look like?

Prayer: *Lord, I ask You to show me what You would like me to fast and for how long. I ask that You would meet me and bring healing and deliverance during this time.*

*Please consult your physician before any type of nutritional fasting.

73

"And if you offer yourselves in compassion for the hungry
and relieve those in misery,
then your dawning light will rise in the darkness
and your gloom will turn into noonday splendor!
Yahweh will always guide you where to go and what to do.
He will fill you with refreshment
even when you are in a dry, difficult place.
He will continually restore strength to you,
so you will flourish like a well-watered garden
and like an ever-flowing, trustworthy spring of blessing.
Your people will rebuild long-deserted ruins,
building anew on foundations laid long before you.
You will be known as Repairers of the Cities
and Restorers of Communities."
Isaiah 58:10-12 (TPT)

These verses continue the fasting theme, emphasizing the other side of the coin. While we deny ourselves, it is critical that we remember charity. These verses are beautiful promises for what a life of generosity looks like. As you heal from your wounds and grow in your relationship with the Lord, this becomes easier and flows more naturally. In the beginning, you were in a terrible place-crushed, broken down and confused. You could barely take care of yourself, let alone anyone else. But as you have walked this walk and seen the Lord provide for you, know that He wants to enable you to begin to help and support others. This may be a financial thing or a practical thing or both! When you turn from your own pain and help to relieve the pain of others, beautiful things are released in the spiritual world. You are promised refreshment, you are promised strength, and you are promised blessing. As you begin to develop generosity, little by little, you will find that the Lord is faithful to give you the strength and provision you require. It becomes Him giving through you, which is such a beautiful process. As you help meet the needs of others, your own needs become abundantly fulfilled.

"The Lord Jesus himself said: 'It is more blessed to give than to receive.'" Acts 20:35b (NIV)

Reflection: Think of a way that you could give today-it could be financial or even giving of your time.

Prayer: *Thank You, Lord, for Your faithfulness to me. Give me the strength and the resources to bless others. Thank You that You will meet all of my needs as I work to help meet the needs of others.*

74

"If you refrain from breaking the Sabbath, from taking your own pleasure on my holy day, if you call the Sabbath 'Delightful', and the day sacred to Yahweh 'Honourable', if you honour it by abstaining from travel, from seeking your own pleasure and from too much talk, 14.then you will find true happiness in Yahweh, and I shall lead you in triumph over the heights of the land. I shall feed you on the heritage of your father Jacob,for the mouth of Yahweh has spoken." Isaiah 58:13-14 (NJB)

In the Old Testament, the Sabbath was considered to be a sacred day where no work was done and the Lord was honored. The Sabbath took place on Saturday. In the New Testament, after Jesus' resurrection on a Sunday, early Christians chose that day as their Sabbath. Walter Elwell writes,

Sabbath contravenes any pride that may accompany human mastery and manipulation of God's creation. In ceasing from labor one is reminded of one's true status as a dependent being, of the God who cares for and sustains all his creatures, and of the world as a reality belonging ultimately to God.[1]

Paul wrote that keeping the Sabbath was not a salvation issue and that it could take place in a variety of forms and didn't necessarily need to be kept on a specific day.

---

1. Elwell, Walter A. "Entry for 'Sabbath." Evangelical Dictionary of Theology-1997.

She is Free Indeed

It is the principal that is of utmost importance. Do we honor God by recognizing our inability to do this life on our own? Do we accept the rest He has ordained for us? When we honor Him in this way, He promises us happiness, or as other versions read, delight, in Him. To enjoy the Lord is to live life honoring His principles.

"Then he said to them, "The Sabbath was made for man, not man for the Sabbath." Mark 2:27 (NIV)

Reflection: What are your practices around the Sabbath? Are they sufficient that you get the rest you need?

Prayer: *Lord, Thank You for the Sabbath rest You ordained for us. Help me to quiet my soul, my mind and my body so that I can fully experience Your rest and find delight in You.*

75

"And this is my covenant promise with them,
says Lord Yahweh.
"From now on, my Holy Spirit will rest on them
and not depart from them,
and my prophetic words will fill their mouths
and will not depart from them, nor from their children,
nor from their descendants, from now on and forever,"
says Lord Yahweh."
Isaiah 59:21 (TPT)

A covenant is also known as an alliance, a pact or a treaty. In Biblical times it was a highly significant and holy agreement made between God and humans. When God gives His word, He never abandons it. And when He places His spirit within you, it will never depart from you, unless of course you reject Him. When Jesus was leaving earth to return to heaven after his resurrection, He told his followers that the experience of the Holy Spirit to come would be even greater than having Him walking the earth with them. That was hard for them to fathom. But on the day of Pentecost, when the Spirit fell, the disciples for the first time experienced what communion with the Lord felt like when it was on a spiritual and not just physical level. Have you been filled with the Spirit? Does the Holy Spirit rest on you?

We need God's Spirit every day. The fruits of the spirit are love, joy, peace, patience, kindness, goodness, gentleness and self control.[1] There is nowhere in the Bible where we are told to try to manufacture these things on our own. They come from the Spirit, not the flesh. Every morning as you wake up, ask the Father to fill you with His Spirit to give you what you need to face the day ahead of you.

"But I tell you the truth, it is to your advantage that I go away; for if I do not go away, the Helper shall not come to you; but if I go, I will send Him to you." John 16:7 (NASB)

Reflection: How do you feel about asking the Holy Spirit to work in your life? Do you believe that He will only do good things?

Prayer: *Thank You, Lord, that You never ask us to do things on our own. Thank You that You are always there, ready to help us. Please send Your Spirit to me right now to fill me up and give me what I need today.*

---

1. *Galations 5:22-23*

76

> *"Rise up in splendor and be radiant, for your light has dawned, and Yahweh's glory now streams from you!*
> *Look carefully! Darkness blankets the earth,*
> *and thick gloom covers the nations,*
> *but Yahweh arises upon you*
> *and the brightness of his glory appears over you!"*
> *Isaiah 60:1-2 (TPT)*

Previously you were living in darkness. The gloom of your partner's power and control cast many shadows over you. When He delivered you, the Lord did not simply remove the darkness and throw away the gloom, but He actually highlighted you. He wants you to lift your head high and walk in the light of His glory. As you take hold of His hand and set your feet to the path that He has set before you, you will begin to glow with His light. Others will see it in you. They will say, "There goes the one God has favored. She who once walked in darkness is now full of light." There will be some who don't see it, who don't believe it. That's okay. Jesus too, was rejected by the majority of the people He came to save.

Remember that you are His chosen daughter. He has appointed you to walk in his light. In a meeting I was once in, Dr Nicholas Catley posed the question, "Is my life's purpose purely for the glory of God?"

She is Free Indeed

Don't let the enemy try to over shadow you by dragging you back into the mire of your previous mistakes, don't let him proclaim darkness over you anymore. You have been set free. Walk in the light.

*"The people living in darkness
have seen a great light;
on those living in the land of the shadow of death
a light has dawned." Matthew 4:16 (NIV)*

Reflection: What does it mean to you to know that you walk in the light?

Prayer: *Thank You, Lord for leading me out of the darkness and into Your everlasting light. Guard my mind from the enemy's attempts to drag me back into the darkness. Shine Your light on me and through me today.*

77

*"The mighty Spirit of Lord Yahweh
is wrapped around me
because Yahweh has anointed me,
as a messenger to preach good news to the poor.
He sent me to heal the wounds of the brokenhearted,
to tell captives, "You are free,"
and to tell prisoners, "Be free from your darkness."
I am sent to announce a new season of Yahweh's grace
and a time of God's recompense on his enemies,
to comfort all who are in sorrow,
to strengthen those crushed by despair who mourn in Zion—
to give them a beautiful bouquet in the place of ashes,
the oil of bliss instead of tears,
and the mantle of joyous praise
instead of the spirit of heaviness.
Because of this, they will be known as
Mighty Oaks of Righteousness,
planted by Yahweh as a living display of his glory."*
Isaiah 61:1-3 (TPT)

This is a Messianic passage. These are such beautiful words about what Jesus came to do. He reaches out to us in the darkness of our prison cells and tells us that He has good news. He has come to set us free and to heal our broken hearts.

Are you walking in a new season of God's grace? Are you accepting the comfort He is offering? Your abusive relationship left you crushed with despair. Do you believe God wants to strengthen you? He truly wants to give you beauty and joy and lightness of spir-

She is Free Indeed

it. He wants His faithfulness to you to be on display. Are you able to embrace these truths today? Do you have faith that God will continue to strengthen and bless you and meet all of your needs? Some days it might be hard to believe. Some days you will want to crawl back into that pit of despair. But your freedom is guaranteed. This is a new season. Things might change slowly, but as you let the Lord work, He will create beauty in your life in ways you could never imagine.

"It is for freedom that Christ has set us free. Stand firm, then, and do not let yourselves be burdened again by a yoke of slavery." Galations 5:1 (NIV)

Reflection: Read the passage in Isaiah aloud. Where it is appropriate, put your name in it.

Prayer: *Jesus, Thank You for my freedom and the beautiful things You have promised me. Help me not to give in to despair but to hold on to my hope in You.*

78

> *"But you will be known as Priests of Yahweh,*
> *and called Servants of our God.*
> *You will feast on the wealth of nations*
> *and revel in their riches!*
> *Because you received a double dose*
> *of shame and dishonor,*
> *you will inherit a double portion*
> *of endless joy and everlasting bliss!*
> *"For I, Yahweh, love fairness and justice,*
> *and I hate stealing and sin.*
> *I will rightly repay them because of my faithfulness*
> *and enter into an everlasting covenant with them."*
> *Isaiah 61:6-8 (TPT)*

Certainly, women who have been abused have received, "a double dose of shame and dishonor." Fairness and justice were denied them. Their dignity, integrity and womanhood were stolen. But do you realize how much the Lord hates what happened to you? He hates it so much that he is ready to give you a double portion in recompense. He wants to demonstrate his faithfulness to you by repaying what you have lost. And he wants to repay you double!

Again, we have the, "already, not yet," idea. The fulness of these promises will be experienced in Heaven, but we can absolutely experience a form of them here on earth. As we enter His presence, we can experience joy and love and total contentment. His covenant with you is everlasting. He will never fail. Let your love for Him be everlasting as well.

Jesus wants you by his side, ministering with Him for eternity. The Passion Translation titles this section of Isaiah 61, "Messiah's Ministers." Jesus calls us, "Servants of our God." Nothing can disqualify you from being a minister of Christ. In fact, he uses our weaknesses to demonstrate his strength. So stand and take your place beside Him. It's the safest place to be.

"For both He who sanctifies and those who are sanctified are all from one Father; for which reason He is not ashamed to call them brethren."
Hebrews 2:11 (NASB)

Reflection: What do you imagine that your, "double portion," will look like?"

Prayer: *Thank You, Jesus, that You call me to be a minister beside You. Help me to remember that I will be repaid for everything that was taken from me. Thank You that You are always faithful.*

79

"I will sing and greatly rejoice in Yahweh!
My whole being vibrates
with shouts of joy in my God!
For he has dressed me with salvation
and wrapped me in the robe of his righteousness!
I appear like a bridegroom on his wedding day,
decked out with a beautiful sash,
or like a radiant bride adorned with sparkling jewels."
Isaiah 61:10 (TPT)

After the promises given in the verses we looked at in the last devotional, the prophet Isaiah bursts with praise. What should our response be when the Holy Spirit teaches or encourages us? It should be praise! There are over 50 references to shouting to the Lord in the Bible. People of our culture will shout over sporting events and concerts, but how often do we actually shout to the Lord? How often do we cheer for Him? The original word in Hebrew in this verse is, *sus*, or *sis*. It means to exult; to rejoice. What would it look like for you to rejoice today? You may be a quiet person; the idea of getting loud might be uncomfortable for you. I would encourage you to push yourself a little today. Take a step toward exuberant rejoicing. The Psalms are full of examples of praise. They include singing, shouting, dancing and playing instruments. It doesn't matter if you have little or even no musical ability-God is listening to your heart. When you take that step of faith and release some of your own inhibitions you will feel that the Lord is near. And as you spend time with Him, He works His healing deep within your soul.

"Shout for joy to the Lord, all the earth. Worship the Lord with gladness; come before him with joyful songs." Psalm 100:1-2 (NIV)

Reflection: What is a new way you can think of to praise the Lord today?

Prayer: *Lord lead me into the fullness of worship today. Help me to put my own self consciousness aside and simply enjoy praising You. I ask that everything else would flee from my mind as I spend time with You.*

80

"I appear like a bridegroom on his wedding day,
decked out with a beautiful sash,
or like a radiant bride adorned with sparkling jewels."
Isaiah 61:10b (TPT)

If you were married to your abusive partner you may cringe at the thought of your wedding or indeed anyone else's. Your wedding anniversary may be a dark day for you. Holidays are also difficult as you spend them alone or only with your immediate family. You may want to crawl into a hole on Valentine's Day. Leaving that relationship often means losing half of your family and losing the traditions that existed around holidays and other special days.

It is interesting that after Isaiah's exuberant praise, he describes himself as someone anticipating his or her wedding day. However, the wedding day Isaiah is referring to is that of the church with Jesus the Messiah. While thinking about your wedding here on earth may cause you pain and despair and even anger, remember that Jesus is coming to take his bride with him to Heaven. Paul writes in Ephesians 5:25 (NIV) "Husbands, love your wives, just as Christ loved the church and gave himself up for her." Your partner did the exact opposite. But Jesus laid Himself down for you. He loves you unconditionally and eternally. You have another wedding ahead of you, but this one will be filled with joy that will last forever!

She is Free Indeed

*"Let us rejoice and exult
and give him the glory,
for the marriage of the Lamb has come,
and his Bride has made herself ready;
8 it was granted her to clothe herself
with fine linen, bright and pure."
Revelation 19:7-8a (ESV)*

Reflection: What do you envision when you think about the Marriage Supper of the Lamb?

Prayer: *Thank You, Lord that You will one day take me home where I belong, with You. Take away the pain from my memories and replace them with joy and excitement for what is to come.*

"For Zion's sake, how can I keep silent?
For Jerusalem's sake, how can I remain quiet?
I will keep interceding until her righteousness
breaks forth like the blazing light of dawn
and her salvation like a burning torch!
Nations will see your victory-vindication,
and every king will witness your blinding radiance!
You will be called by a brand-new name,
given to you from the mouth of Yahweh himself.
You will be a beautiful crown held high in the hand of Yahweh,
a royal crown of splendor
held in the open palm of your God!"
Isaiah 62:1-3 (TPT)

While these verses refer to the nation of Israel, we as believers have been adopted into the nation of Israel by God our Father.

God is not silent about your trials. He is not watching passively from his throne in heaven. He is actively interceding for you. While it is important to remember is that He rarely overrides free will, He is always working on our behalf. And He promises to keep working until your righteousness "breaks forth like the blazing light of dawn." Your redemption is in process, and the cumulation will be that you will shine brightly and beautifully. Everyone will see that you have been redeemed and vindicated. You will be held high in the hand of God.

She is Free Indeed

Your former partner most likely lives in denial. You may think that justice will never come for what he has done to you. While we do not know the mind of God, nor can we accurately predict His judgement, we can be assured that those men will one day fully realize what they have done. All will be revealed. So keep your eyes on that beautiful crown of splendor that will one day be yours.

"And we know that God causes all things to work together for good to those who love God, to those who are called according to His purpose."
Romans 8:28 (NASB)

Reflection: How does knowing what the future looks like help you in your trials today?

Prayer: *Thank You Lord for Your continued work on my behalf. Thank You that one day Your justice will be full and complete. Thank You that one day I will be completely healed and restored and vindicated!*

*"I will tell again of the faithful, gracious acts of Yahweh
and praise him for everything he has done for us—
the wonderful goodness, the riches of his mercy,
which he has shown to the house of Israel,
and the abundance of his endless love."
Isaiah 63:7 (TPT)*

These verses are encouraging us to give testimony to what God has done for us. Isaiah 62:4-12 continues with the theme of God's mighty deliverance. Isaiah 62:11a (TPT),

"See? Yahweh has proclaimed to the ends of the earth:
Tell my daughter, Zion,
"Look, here comes your Deliverer!"

And in 62:12 (TPT),
"They will be called His Holy People,
The Redeemed of Yahweh.
And you will be known as Those Whom God Loves,
A City Not Abandoned."

The Lord has been so gracious to us, He has taken all of our sin and shame upon Himself. He has been so good and merciful to us, taking us out of our destructive relationships. His love is endless. So tell your story. Share your testimony. Give Him the praise for what He has done. When others praise your bravery and strength, point them to Jesus, your source. When others ask you how you did it, how you escaped, point to Jesus your deliverer. When others ask for your advice, point them to Jesus, the source of your wisdom. When others ask you how you are managing to hold on, point them to Jesus, the One who will never abandon you. Tell everyone of His endless love.

"He brought them out of darkness and the shadow of death, And broke their chains in pieces." Psalm 107:14 (NKJ)

Reflection: What is something that the Lord has done in your life that you could share with someone today?

Prayer: *Thank You, Lord for all that You have done for me. Give me opportunities to share my testimony with others. Make me an encouragement to the people around me every day.*

"For he said, 'Truly they are my people, children who will not betray me,' and he became their Saviour. 9.In all their troubles, it was no messenger or angel but his presence that saved them. In his love and pity he himself redeemed them, lifted them up and carried them throughout the days of old."
Isaiah 63:8-9 (NJB)

This chapter refers to God's deliverance of the nation of Israel. Never forget that it was the Lord who delivered you. He sent you helpers and He gave you wisdom and strength to do what seemed impossible. Yet there are still many battles ahead. And unfortunately, you will not win all of them. When you face a defeat, a defeat that makes you question God, a defeat when you were expecting a win, you may be devastated. You may question God's power as it may have seemed like a battle God could easily have won for you. Don't let the enemy tempt you in those times to betray God, to turn your back on Him.

Every time the Israelites faced a new obstacle in their journey towards the promised land, they doubted the Lord. They forgot the all of the incredible miracles He had already done for them.

It is so human to experience a defeat and think that the Lord has forgotten you. The Passion Translation of verse 9 says, "When they suffered, he suffered with them." God limits Himself in order protect our freedom of choice. So not every battle on this earth is won. But the *war* has been won. In those crushing moments, instead of shaking a fist at God, raise up open hands instead and ask Him what He is going to do with this loss in order to redeem it.

"Surely the arm of the LORD is not too short to save, nor his ear too dull to hear." Isaiah 59:1 (NIV)

Reflection: Look back on a recent defeat. Ask the Lord how He is going to redeem it for you.

Prayer: *Lord help me never to forget all of the things You have done for me. Help me to keep my eyes on You when everything around me is falling apart. Help me to hold firmly to my faith.*

❊ 84 ❊

"Yet still, Yahweh, you are our Father.
We are like clay and you are our Potter.
Each one of us is the creative, artistic work of your hands"
Isaiah 64:8 (TPT)

For someone who has experienced a lot of trauma, this verse can provoke worry and even be triggering. We don't want anymore molding, shaping or refining. We feel we have been through the fire too many times!

It's important to recognize that the potter can only work with the clay he or she has been given. And the purpose is to create something beautiful. While the Lord is shaping us, the enemy loves to try to ruin us. Clay that is too dry is difficult to work with. The enemy loves to try to harden our hearts. Clay can sometimes have air pockets that cause it to be misshapen. The enemy loves to plant seeds of doubt in our minds. Clay needs a certain amount of water to be shaped properly. The enemy likes to turn our minds away from the Spirit, our source of the water of life. Clay can also be too wet. The enemy loves to mess with our mental health and leave us emotionally overwrought and exhausted. Clay must be worked with gently, too much force and it will be off center. The enemy loves to throw any kind of trial against us, to take us off center. If the pottery wheel is going too slow, the clay will not stay centered. The enemy loves to try to overwhelm and exhaust us. If the potter lets go, the clay will fly around haphazardly. This can happen when we believe the enemy's lies and turn away from the Lord. Remember that the Potter is creating something beautiful. Trust Him every moment.

"Being confident of this, that he who began a good work in you will carry it on to completion until the day of Christ Jesus." Philippians 1:6 (NIV)

Reflection: Think about your heart. Is there a way you could open it more to the Lord?

Prayer: *Thank You, Lord that You are creating something beautiful out of my life. When things become painful and difficult, help me to remember that the enemy is the one trying to thwart the process. Thank You that You will be faithful to complete it.*

*"Look! I am creating
entirely new heavens and a new earth!
They will be so wonderful
that no one will even think about the old ones anymore!
As you wait for the reality of what I am creating,
be filled with joy and unending gladness!
Look! I am ready to create Jerusalem
as a source of sheer joy,
and her people, an absolute delight!
I will rejoice in this new Jerusalem
and find great delight in my people.
You will no longer hear
the sound of weeping or cries of distress."
Isaiah 65:17-19 (TPT)*

There are over 600 references to heaven in the Bible. Yet you rarely hear a sermon about heaven. God does not want us to be as focused as we are on this earth. He wants us to put our hope not in our financial future, or our health or our family. He wants us to put our hope in our eternal future-the one in His glorious presence. It will be so incredible that we won't even remember what we faced on this earth. That seems so impossible right now doesn't it? And yet the contrast between earth and heaven will be so great that no evil thing that happened here on earth will even cross our minds anymore. And while we will be filled with joy and unending gladness then, these verses say that we can have that even now as we wait

She is Free Indeed

for eternity. The joy can begin today. The never-ending gladness can already be in our hearts.

Take heart, as you cry and weep because of your pain on this earth. While things feel intense and overwhelming, the time is coming where you will never cry or weep again.

"So we fix our eyes not on what is seen, but on what is unseen, since what is seen is temporary, but what is unseen is eternal." 2 Corinthians 4:18 (NIV)

Reflection: Think about an area in your life where you are struggling. It could be something like fear or physical pain. Now imagine how different that problem will be in Heaven.

Prayer: *Lord help me to fix my eyes on You. Help me to remember every day that Heaven is my future; help me to access that joy and gladness even now through my suffering.*

86

"Thus says Yahweh: With heaven my throne and earth my footstool, what house could you build me, what place for me to rest, 2.when all these things were made by me and all belong to me? - declares Yahweh. But my eyes are drawn to the person of humbled and contrite spirit, who trembles at my word...5. Listen to the word of Yahweh, you who tremble at his word. Your brothers, who hate and reject you because of my name, have said, 'Letah̄-weh show his glory, let us witness your joy!' But they will be put to shame."
Isaiah 66:1-2, 5 (NJB)

One of the common forms of domestic abuse is spiritual abuse. You may have lived with someone who was not a Christian who mocked you because of your faith. He may have belittled your devotion to the Lord. Or you may have lived with someone who professed to be a Christian who used the Bible as a weapon against you. He may have challenged the authenticity of your faith as he put the blame for troubles in the marriage on you.

But what kind of person does the Lord make His home in? He makes his home in the hearts of the humble and contrite, in the ones who respect His word. He does not make His home in the proud or the harsh. He does not make His home in someone who would use His holy words to harm another.

The taunt at the end of this passage is ironic because that is exactly what the Lord will do if you let him. He will show His glory through you and He will pour His joy out upon you. Your delight in Him will be your vindication. His faithfulness to you will be your testimony.

"God blesses those who are humble, for they will inherit the whole earth." Matthew 5:5 (NLT)

Reflection: How has your relationship with God been used against you?

Prayer: *Lord, come and make Your home in me. Reveal Your glory in and to me and give me Your joy. Let Your faithfulness to me be my testimony as I share Your love with others.*

87

"For Yahweh says:
"I will extend to her prosperity like a river
and the wealth of gentiles like a flooding river.
You will nurse from her breast, be cradled in her arms,
and delightfully bounced on her knees. As a mother tenderly comforts her child,
so will I tenderly comfort you,
and you will find comfort in Jerusalem."
Isaiah 66:12-13 (TPT)

God is most often portrayed as a father in scrip-tu re. But as we were made in God's image, male and female, he has a mother side as well. We see that in these verses. It is an unfortunate fact that abuse tends to repeat itself generationally. It is not uncommon for a woman who is abused by her partner to have been abused by one or both her own parents as well. There may well be a little girl inside you who was never lovingly parented as described in the verses above. You need to know that that was not God's plan for you and it breaks His heart when His plan for family was so horribly twisted.

Know that you can bring that little girl before the Lord so that He can pour out both his mother and father love on you. What safer place is there for a baby than when held in their mother's arms nursing? What more joyful place than being bounced in the lap of a loving parent? When a child is hurt, they run to their parents for comfort. God is longing for you to run to him for tender comfort today. He alone is trustworthy.

*"As a father has compassion on his children,
so the Lord has compassion on those who fear him."
Psalm 103:13 (NIV)*

Reflection: How do you see the Lord working in your life both as a mother and a father?

Prayer: *Thank You, Lord, that You are the perfect parent. Thank You that I can bring my hurts and my pain before You and You will always tenderly comfort me. I bring You my broken heart today and ask you for Your healing.*

88

"This is what I shall keep in mind and so regain some hope: 22.Surely Yahweh's mercies are not over, his deeds of faithful love not exhausted; 23.every morning they are renewed; great is his faithfulness! 24.'Yahweh is all I have,' I say to myself, 'and so I shall put my hope in him.' 25.Yahweh is good to those who trust him, to all who search for him. 26.It is good to wait in silence for Yahweh to save." Lamentations 3:21-26 (NJB)

These verses are found in the middle of the prophet Jeremiah's 3rd lament. Jeremiah had some pretty good reasons for being utterly miserable. He was God's appointed prophet and yet he had been dreadfully persecuted and no one believed his words. Yet this is what he held on to-he knew that his God would never fail. He knew that the only thing he had to hold onto was his faith in a God who is good and trustworthy. The Lord is found by all those who eagerly and earnestly seek Him.

The final sentence of this passage is profound. "It is good to wait in silence for Yahweh to save." What can this mean but that there are times when we need to stand down, when we need to let go of everything we are fighting for, when we need to step aside so that the Lord can do His work. It is absolutely a test of faith. The word, "wait," is important here. God's timing is rarely what we think it should be. And yet waiting for His way is always the best decision. His timing always produces the best outcome. So keep your heart open to hear what the Lord is saying. And if He asks you to step aside for a time and let Him work, trust that He knows what He's doing.

I believe that I shall look upon the goodness of the Lord in the land of the living! Wait for the Lord; be strong, and let your heart take courage; wait for the Lord!" Psalm 27:13-14 (ESV)"

Reflection: What is the Lord asking you to let go of today?

Prayer: *Lord, You are all I have. Thank You that you are always working and always faithful. Help me to know when I need to stand down, to put my plans and thoughts aside and let You do the work. I put all of my hope in You today.*

❋ 89 ❋

"They shut me finally in a pit, they closed me in with a stone. 54. The waters rose over my head; I thought, 'I am lost!' 55. Yahweh, I called on your name from the deep pit. 56. You heard my voice, do not close your ear to my prayer, to my cry. 57. You are near when I call to you. You said, 'Do not be afraid!'"
Lamentations 3:53-57 (NJB)

This passage is not figurative. Jeremiah was literally tossed into a pit filled with mud. There was no drinkable water and no food. Jeremiah had prophesied and the King of Judah was angry. When Jeremiah called out to the Lord, God told him not to be afraid. And yet he was still in the pit, hungry, thirsty and miserable. While he assumed he would die there, God was working on a plan to get him out. While the Bible does not tell us exactly how long he was in there, he was eventually saved.

When you are stuck in a pit, with destruction hovering over you; when all hope is lost, call upon the Lord. He will hear you. He is near. And He will tell you not to be afraid. He may not rescue you right away. You might be stuck there for a while. But as he told Jeremiah not to be afraid, so He says to you as well. How absurd! How can peace be found when you are in the dark, surrounded by mud, hungry, thirsty, afraid of drowning and death with no one left to help you? It can only be found when you call out to the Lord, when He is near and when He speaks His peace over you.

She is Free Indeed

*"When I am afraid, I put my trust in you.
In God, whose word I praise—
in God I trust and am not afraid.
What can mere mortals do to me?" Psalm
56: 3-4 (NIV)*

Reflection: How have you held on to your faith in God when you have been in the pit of despair?

Prayer: *Lord, when I am afraid, help me to remember to call on You. I Thank You that no matter what situation I am in, You are near. Help me to trust when everything around me is falling apart. Thank You that You have a plan for my deliverance.*

90

"If our God, the one we serve, is able to save us from the burning fiery furnace and from your power, Your Majesty, he will save us; 18.and even if he does not, then you must know, Your Majesty, that we will not serve your god or worship the statue you have set up.'" Daniel 3:17-18 (NJB)

We revisit the story around these verses which is that of Shadrach, Meshach and Abednego. They were Jews living in captivity in Babylon. The Babylonian king, Nebuchadnezzar, had set up an idol and commanded the people to bow to it. These three men were devout followers of God and refused to bow. They were told that if they did not, they would be thrown into a fiery furnace and burned to death.

There are five words in this passage that are some of the most profound and faith filled in all of scripture: "even if he does not." These 3 men were so devoted to the Lord, that even if the Lord did not come through for them in the way they hoped, they still pledged to trust and serve Him.

While we pray and have faith and hope in the Lord, we need to realize that not all of our problems are going to be resolved the way we want them to be. We live on a fallen planet where most people reject Jesus the Messiah. Not everything is going to be resolved perfectly this side of eternity. We are still going to struggle on this earth. But we are never left alone.

She is Free Indeed

"And we know that for those who love God all things work together for good, for those who are called according to his purpose." Romans 8:28 (ESV)

Reflection: If you face loss and disappointment, if you face betrayal and rejection-are you still prepared to stay surrendered to Jesus?

Prayer: *Lord, I Thank You that Heaven is my home. Help me to have peace even when things go terribly wrong here on earth, knowing that You have my back and that You will work everything out in the end.*

91

"He is the living God, he endures for ever, his kingdom will never be destroyed and his empire never come to an end. 28.He saves, sets free, and works signs and wonders in the heavens and on earth."
Daniel 6:27b-28a (NJB)

Without the context of the surrounding verses, these words sound like they come from the Psalms. But ironically, they are actually the words of Darius, one of the kings of Babylon. Before he wrote these words, Darius actually considered himself to be a deity worthy of praise.

Darius' transformation took place after the famous story of Daniel in the lions' den. In short, King Darius had decreed that anyone who prayed to any god other than himself should be thrown into a den of hungry lions. Daniel, who served the Most High God, was unwilling to turn his back on God or even hide his devotion. He was therefore sentenced to death by lions. However, God closed the mouths of those lions and Daniel miraculously survived. Note that God did not do anything miraculous to spare Daniel from spending the night in that dark reeking cave filled with vicious lions. In the morning, the King, who actually strongly respected Daniel, went to discover that Daniel had survived. It was after this that he proclaimed the words in the verses above. The fact that Daniel had survived convinced the king of the sovereignty of God.

She is Free Indeed

You, too, escaped a metaphoric lions' den. You survived; you were not eaten up. Your story will also be one that will convince others of the sovereignty of God. Be prepared to share it.

"King Darius then wrote to all nations, peoples and languages dwelling throughout the world: 'May you prosper more and more! 27. This is my decree: Throughout every dominion of my realm, let all tremble with fear before the God of Daniel.'" Daniel 6:26-27a (NJB)

Reflection: How was Daniel's experience similar to your own?

Prayer: *Thank You, Lord, that You did not leave me to be devoured. I ask that You would give me opportunities to share my story that others could believe and be saved.*

92

"I am God, not man, the Holy One in your midst, and I shall not come to you in anger." Hosea 11:9b (NJB)

This declaration by God is made in the midst of his complaints about the faithlessness of Israel. Hosea the prophet was actually compelled by God to marry an adulterous woman and raise her illegitimate children as a metaphor for God's relationship with the nation of Israel. There are harsh words throughout this book of the Bible. God talks of Israel's great wickedness, crimes and guilt. They turned their backs on him and violated his gracious covenant over and over. He talks about how he loved and cared for them tenderly, but now he plans to slaughter them. But then He stops His rant. He realizes that He does not want to come to His people in harshness and anger. In his wrath, he remembers mercy.[1]

These words were written before Jesus' sacrifice made atonement for all of the sin of humankind, in the past, present and the future. People wonder how to compare the God of the Old Testament with the God of the New Testament. God didn't change. His love remained the same. In the Old Testament, people had to pay the price for their sins themselves. In the New Testament we are offered unconditional for-

---

1. *(Habakkuk 3:2).*

giveness based only on our acceptance of it. In these verses we see that the true heart of God was not really to punish his people. He loved them dearly.

God never comes to you in anger. He comes to you with love and unfailing patience. Don't let the enemy make you afraid of God. He is never waiting to judge you in anger, He is always waiting to forgive and restore.

"Ephraim, how could I part with you? Israel how could I give you up?" Hosea 11:8a (NJB)

Reflection: Do you ever feel like the Lord is angry with you? How do these verses help you with that feeling?

Prayer: *Thank You Lord that Your love never ceases. Thank You that You have patience and that You don't get angry with me. Help me to trust that I can come to you with anything at anytime, anywhere.*

93

"But I have been Yahweh your God since your days in Egypt when you knew no god but me, since you had no one else to save you. 5.I cared for you in the desert, in the land of dreadful drought. 6.I pastured them, and they were satisfied; once satisfied, their hearts grew proud, and therefore they forgot me."
Hosea 13:4-6 (NJB)

In the time of chaos, you learn to lean on the Lord, you know that only He can help you. Once you get back on your feet again and start to feel stronger, it is easy to start relying on yourself and forgetting the true source of your strength. The trouble is that once you start to do this, you find your strength and hope starting to ebb away. It happens gradually, such that you don't even notice it until you are once again facing a pit of despair. Charles Spurgeon writes, "We must value Him as our best treasure; we must prize His words and His ordinances; and we must keep our thoughts of Him and knowledge of Him under lock and key, lest the devil should steal anything from us."[1]

It is easy to condemn the Israelites of that, because over and over they forgot what the Lord had done for them and became fearful and doubted Him. But we are just as guilty. When we face a new challenge, a new battle, we once again become afraid and overwhelmed. But the good news is that it's never too late. God created us and He understands our weaknesses. He is always there, waiting for us to turn back

---

1. *Morning and Evening April 13* Public domain

She is Free Indeed

and hold our hands out to Him once again.

"So turn back with God's help, maintain faithful love and loyalty and always put your trust in your God." Hosea 12:7 (NJB)

Reflection: How many times have you forgotten about God? What action can you take today to lean on Him?

Prayer: *Lord forgive me when I lose sight of You, when I start to trust in my own strength and abilities. I turn to You today and ask You for the strength I need.*

94

> *"Be glad, people of Zion,*
> *rejoice in the Lord your God,*
> *for he has given you the autumn rains*
> *because he is faithful.*
> *He sends you abundant showers,*
> *both autumn and spring rains, as before.*
> *The threshing floors will be filled with grain;*
> *the vats will overflow with new wine and oil."*
> *Joel 2:23-24 (NIV)*

Autumn rains are incredibly important. They end the drought of summer and soften hardened ground. They are the "early" rains that come before the "latter" rains of spring. These rains signal to farmers that the cycle of life continues. There is a Jewish holiday in the fall called *Sukkot*. It is a celebration of the harvest and also commemorates the Israelites' freedom from Egypt. In North America we also celebrate Thanksgiving in the fall.

The Lord has been faithful to you. He led you out of Egypt, out of the dry desert. As you walk your journey of freedom, He promises you both the autumn rains and the spring rains. Our lives have seasons just as the earth does. There are dry periods and there are periods full of life. When you enter the winter or the summer seasons of your life, remember that fall and spring are coming. He will pour out His rain on your dry and weary soul. He will awaken the things that lie dormant in the winter. You will see fruit in your life. Make sure you have room on your threshing floors and in your vats for His abundance. Be open and ready for His blessing.

"You Heavens above, rain down my righteousness; let the clouds shower it down. Let the earth open wide, let salvation spring up, let righteousness flourish with it; I, the LORD, have created it." Isaiah 45:8 (NIV)

Reflection: Look back on your own, "seasons." How has the Lord provided even in the desert?

Prayer: *Thank You Lord for always bringing refreshment and blessing. Help me to prepare my heart to receive it so that I can flourish as Your child.*

95

"Then I will make up to you for the years
That the swarming locust has eaten,
The creeping locust, the stripping locust and the gnawing locust,
My great army which I sent among you.
"You will have plenty to eat and be satisfied
And praise the name of the Lord your God,
Who has dealt wondrously with you;
Then My people will never be put to shame.
"Thus you will know that I am in the midst of Israel,
And that I am the Lord your God,
And there is no other;
And My people will never be put to shame."
Joel 2:25-27 (NASB)

Joel is a book about God's judgement on Israel. God's people had turned their backs on Him so many times. He was, quite literally, fed up with them. But again, in wrath, he remembers mercy. Locust first appeared in the Bible as one of the plagues God sent against the Egyptians when they were holding Israel in captivity. There are several types of locust mentioned in this passage. The Hebrew words for them are all different, but the direct translations are not completely clear. However, it is easy to compare the different types of locust with what your former partner did to you. He swarmed you-he gaslighted you, making you question your sanity. He messed with your head. The abuse didn't all begin at once, it began quietly, creeping up on you. He then stripped you-of your beliefs about yourself, possibly about your beliefs about your family and friends, and he stripped you of your dignity. The gnawing locust ate away at your soul, at your identity.

But the good news is that no matter what he did to you, the Lord is going to heal you. He is going to make up for it. You will be repaid and vindicated. And not only that, but He is going to bless you beyond measure.

"Instead of your shame you will receive a double portion, and instead of disgrace you will rejoice in your inheritance. And so you will inherit a double portion in your land, and everlasting joy will be yours." Isaiah 61:7 (NIV)

Reflection: Begin now to keep track of the ways the Lord is restoring to you the times in your life that locust have eaten.

Prayer: *Thank You, Lord, that You have promised me restoration. I ask that You heal and rebuild my soul and that I would never be ashamed again.*

96

"Seek good and not evil so that you may survive, and Yahweh, God Sabaoth, be with you as you claim he is. 15.Hate evil, love good, let justice reign at the city gate: it may be that Yahweh, God Sabaoth, will take pity on the remnant of Joseph." Amos 5:14-15 (NJB)

God is just. He longs for justice on this earth. Do you seek out good? Do you hate evil? While the earth is filled with beauty and wonderful things, it is also filled with injustice. The Lord calls us to act when we see injustice. If you are wondering what God's will is for you-look around and see what God is doing and join in! When Jesus left His disciples to ascend to Heaven, he told them to be His witnesses in Judea, Samaria and to the ends of the earth. Judea was their immediate surroundings. Samaria was the larger region. We are called to our own cities, our own states and provinces, our own countries and also to the whole world. There is no lack of need, there are limitless charities and organizations that you can donate to or be a part of. Perhaps God is calling you to work with and encourage women in your community who have also experienced abusive relationships. In 2 Corinthians 1:4 (NIV) Paul writes about Jesus, " who comforts us in all our troubles, so that we can comfort those in any trouble with the comfort we ourselves receive from God." What greater ministry than to encourage people with your own life story, with your own testimony?

She is Free Indeed

"For just as we share abundantly in the sufferings of Christ, so also our comfort abounds through Christ. 6 If we are distressed, it is for your comfort and salvation; if we are comforted, it is for your comfort, which produces in you patient endurance of the same sufferings we suffer."
2 Corinthians 1:5-6 (NIV)

Reflection: What action could you take today to help bring justice in your community?

Prayer: *Thank You, Lord for what You have done in my life. Show me opportunities to work for justice and to comfort others who have experienced the same things I have.*

97

"This is what he showed me: the Lord standing by a wall, with a plumb-line in His hand. 8.'What do you see, Amos?' Yahweh asked me. 'A pl umb- line,' I said. Then the Lord said, 'Look, I am going to put a plumb-line in among my people Israel; never again will I overlook their offences."
Amos 7:7-8 (NJB)

A plumb line is often used in construction to ensure that vertical planes are exact. In other words, is something standing straight without leaning to the right or the left? A plumb line is exacting. It allows for no deviation. In these verses, the Lord had decided in judgment that He would never overlook sin again.

That sounds daunting. How are we to be perfect? The good news is that Jesus is our plumb line. When the Father looks at us, He sees Jesus' perfection. When we surrender our lives to Jesus, we become clothed in His righteousness. Our sins are covered; past, present and future. When God held up the plumb line, no one passed the test. He knew He needed a way to change that and He ultimately decided to do the opposite of what He said in these verses. He has overlooked our offences. But there was a cost. Jesus had to take all of those offences upon Himself and He had to face all of the consequences of our sin. It was a weighty thing which we should never take lightly. We must do our best to love God and to love all of His creation. While we indeed have a get out of jail free card, we should treat it with utmost respect and gratefulness.

"Come now, let's settle this," says the LORD. "Though your sins are like scarlet, I will make them as white as snow. Though they are red like crimson, I will make them as white as wool." Isaiah 1:18 (NLT)

Reflection: Are you still holding on to guilt and shame? Can you accept the Lord's complete and total forgiveness today?

Prayer: *Thank You Lord, for seeing my sin through the blood of Jesus. Thank You, Jesus, for Your tremendous sacrifice. May my life glorify You because of all You have done for me.*

98

"He has shown you, O mortal, what is good. And what does the LORD require of you? To act justly and to love mercy and to walk humbly with your God." Micah 6:8 (NIV)

This verse is beautiful in its simplicity. All of the law and requirements in the Bible can be boiled down to these words. To "act justly," is also translated, to do what is right, to promote justice or to see that justice is done. The Lord wants us to seek justice, to seek what is right for all of His people. When you see an injustice, do what you can to act. This may be as simple as feeding a homeless person, or could be as big as founding a charity. Keep your eyes open to injustice and your heart soft to hearing the Father's words about it.

"To love mercy," is also translated as to love kindness or to love goodness. This flows naturally from seeking justice. Pay attention to everyone you see. Each one is a beloved child of the Father. Purpose your heart toward kindness and generosity.

Most versions translate the last phrase as "walk humbly with your God." The Good News translation says to, "live in humble fellowship with God." Again, this is simple. Every day we open our hearts to the Lord and ask Him what He wants to teach us and how He wants to use us. We recognize our own inability to live without Him and His strength. And then we watch and see what He will do through us.

"Jesus replied: "'Love the Lord your God with all your heart and with all your soul and with all your mind. This is the first and greatest commandment. And the second is like it: 'Love your neighbor as yourself.'"
Matthew 22:37-39 (NIV)

Reflection: How could you love your neighbor today?

Prayer: *Lord, show me today where I can show mercy, where I can demonstrate kindness. Show me how I can pursue justice for Your children. I come humbly before You, acknowledging that I have nothing without You, but with You I have everything.*

99

"Do not gloat over me, my enemy: though I have fallen, I shall rise; though I live in darkness, Yahweh is my light." Micah 7:8 (NJB)

Whether you could see it or not, your partner spent your relationship gloating over you. Other versions use the words, "don't rejoice over me." Narcissists feed off of traumatizing their victims. Every time your face looked fearful or confused, every time you doubted yourself or questioned your judgment because of what he said, every time you caved to his demands, he indeed rejoiced. Those were all little victories for him.

But though you had fallen, Yahweh came into that dark, empty place. He shone His eternal light on you and raised you up again. As you go through the process of extricating yourself completely from that relationship, there will still be times when your former partner feels like he has won victories and he will gloat. You will feel like you have fallen right back into that dark, frightening place all over again. But know that each and every time, your God will shine His light of favor on you and He will lift you up. Over and over, no matter how many times your enemy knocks you down, the Lord will restore you. The day will come when you are on your feet permanently, when your enemy is completely defeated and he will gloat no more over you. Hold tight to your coming victory.

She is Free Indeed

"In my distress I called to the LORD; I cried to my God for help. From His temple he heard my voice; my cry came before Him, into His ears." Psalm 18:6 (NIV)

Reflection: Picture yourself standing in light today. Listen to what the Lord tells you.

Prayer: *Lord, Thank You that You are my light and my salvation. Thank You for always come to my rescue. Help me to hold onto the victory I have in You every day.*

❋ 100 ❋

"O LORD, I have heard of what you have done, and I am filled with awe. Now do again in our times the great deeds you used to do. Be merciful, even when you are angry." Habakkuk 3:2 (GNT)

Genesis 4:26 (NIV) "At that time people began to call on the name of the LORD." From the beginning of time, God's people have called and cried out to Him, recognizing their own weaknesses and incapability. In the verse above, the prophet Habakkuk calls out to the Lord. Habakkuk knew what the Lord had done thus far in history. He praised the Lord for His might and His power. He called on the Lord to act once again. He looked around Him and saw devastation and judgment. He asked the Lord to remember mercy in His anger.

This is not just an Old Testament concept. Today we still need to call on the Lord, we still need to cry out to Him. We need to thankfully acknowledge everything he has done for us. We need to ask Him to demonstrate His mercy.

Are you fearful? Call on the name of the Lord!
Are you tired? Call on the name of the Lord!
Are you facing a critical decision? Call on the name of the Lord!
Are you lonely and hurting? Call on the name of the Lord!

She is Free Indeed

Is your trauma being triggered? Call on the name of the Lord!

No matter what your issue is today, you can call on the Lord.

"Because He has inclined His ear to me, Therefore I shall call upon Him as long as I live."
Psalm 116:2 (NASB)

Reflection: What are some specific things you need to call on the Lord for today?

Prayer: *Lord I cry out to You today. Please come and deliver me from all of my distress. Show me Your mercy and help me in my time of need.*

❋ 101 ❋

"But I shall rejoice in Yahweh, I shall exult in God my Saviour. 19. Yahweh my Lord is my strength, he will make my feet as light as a doe's, and set my steps on the heights." Habakkuk 3:18-19a (NJB)

These verses come at the end of the book of the prophet Habakkuk. The book is mostly about the Lord's judgment. This last chapter is a prayer but is also written as a song. In the midst of a nation in rebellion against the Lord, the prophet takes time to worship. He rejoices, he exults. He sings of the strength of Yahweh. Somehow in the middle of such heaviness, Habakkuk says that the Lord makes his feet light like a deer. Have you ever seen a prancing deer? Not even the most talented of dancers can mimic the way a deer is light on its feet. And when they dance about, they dance joyfully, with abandon.

You too, have been surrounded with heaviness and your feet have trod the depths of the earth. If this joy, this lightness, this elevation of circumstances was available to Habakkuk, it is also available to you. Other versions, in the middle of verse 19 say, "walk upon the high hills." God does not expect you to climb those mountains on your own. Just as He does for the deer, He is the one who is going to provide the strength, He is going to shore up your tired feet. In the middle of your struggle, God is right there with you.

She is Free Indeed

"God is our refuge and strength, an ever-present help in trouble."
Psalm 46:1 (NIV)

Reflection: List the ways the Lord is helping you on your journey.

> **Prayer:** *Thank You, Lord, that You are my strength when I am weak and that You give me what I need to make it through every day. Help me to feel light on my feet with Your strength today.*

102

"When that Day comes, the message for Jerusalem will be: Zion, have no fear, do not let your hands fall limp. 17. Yahweh your God is there with you, the warrior-Saviour. He will rejoice over you with happy song, he will renew you by His love, he will dance with shouts of joy for you."
Zephaniah 3:16-17 (NJB)

These are such beautiful verses that demonstrate how much the Lord loves us. Can you imagine Him singing over you because He loves you so much? Can you imagine Him dancing over you? Nowhere else in Scripture do we find a better expression of the delight the Lord has in His children. While Zephaniah is again a book written by a prophet filled with judgment and doom, the last half of the last chapter is a promise of hope to come.

How do we keep our hands from going limp? By raising them up to the Father so that He can give them His strength. He is our, "warrior Saviour." Not only has he saved us, he also actively fights for us! Some days it's hard to imagine anyone actually rejoicing over us. But He does. His love is enough to completely renew us. What would be the words be to His song over you? What would His joyful dance steps look like? What would His shouts over you sound like? I would encourage you to ask the Lord those questions today. He wants you to know the worth you have in Him and how much He completely adores you.

She is Free Indeed

"And may you have the power to understand, as all God's people should, how wide, how long, how high, and how deep His love is."
Ephesians 3:18 (NLT)

Reflection: Write down what the Lord reveals to you about the ways He rejoices over you.

Prayer: *Lord reveal your love for me today. Help me to hear the words that You sing and shout over me. Help me to see the delight of Your dance over me. Thank You for Your unending love.*

❈ 103 ❈

"It happened at that time that the Philistines mustered to make war on Israel... The Philistines drew up their battle-line against Israel, the fighting was fierce, and Israel was beaten by the Philistines: about four thousand men in their ranks were killed on the field of battle. When the troops returned to camp, the elders of Israel said, 'Why haYahweh caused us to be beaten by the Philistines today? Let us fetch the ark of our God from Shiloh so that, when it goes with us, it may save us from the clutches of our enemies.'"1 Samuel 4: 1b-3 (NJB)

The Israelites were once again facing war. Many were not serving Yahweh anymore. The priest at the time, Eli, was weak spiritually and his 2 sons were called, "scoundrels." Facing defeat, the Israelites made a fatal mistake. Ignoring all of the law regarding the temple and the ark of the covenant, they took that ark out of the temple and into battle with them. This was extraordinarily irreverent. They were hoping for the ark to act like a talisman. They thought it held a certain degree of luck. It did not, and it was captured by the Philistines. Instead of inquiring of the Lord, the Israelites went off on their own, thinking what had worked in the past should work now. They did not even consult the high priest.

We must be careful not to assume what God's will is, or what He would have us do in a certain situation. Just because he has led us one way in the past, that does not mean he wants us to do the same thing in the future. It is critically important that we always ask for the Lord's leading. Never take a step without consulting the King.

"Your word is a lamp for my feet, a light on my path."
Psalm 119:105 (NIV)

Reflection: Where have you struggled in the past when you did not seek the Lord's leading?

Prayer: *Lord I ask you to lead me. Help me not to take a step without asking for Your light to illuminate the path You want me to take.*

104

"And Yahweh my God will come, and all the holy ones with Him. 6. That Day, there will be no light, but only cold and frost. 7. And it will be one continuous day -- Yahweh knows -- there will be no more day and night, and it will remain light right into the time of evening. 8. When that Day comes, living waters will issue from Jerusalem, half towards the eastern sea, half towards the western sea; they will flow summer and winter. 9. Then Yahweh will become king of the whole world. When that Day comes, Yahweh will be the one and only and His name the one name." Zechariah 14:5b-9 (NJB)

These verses speak of the final judgment. A long day of darkness, cold and frost. We are not told in these verses what specifically occurs on that day, but it must mean that the Lord deals with the deeds of darkness once and for all, because after that day, there is only light. Revelation 22:5b (NIV) describes it as, "They will not need the light of a lamp or the light of the sun, for the Lord God will give them light." No darkness. No more hiding. No more fear. No more evil. No more worrying about what tomorrow might bring.

There are dozens of references to living water throughout both the Old and New Testaments. This water refers to the outpouring of the Spirit of God. While we can experience the life this bring us here on earth, these verses describe a free, ever flowing abundance in every season, available to all who come to drink or bathe in it. All judgment will be over as Yahweh will be the only name, the king of everything.

She is Free Indeed

That day is known only to God the Father. But it is coming. And He is eagerly anticipating it even more than we can imagine.

"And all drank the same spiritual drink. For they drank from the spiritual Rock that followed them, and the Rock was Christ."
1 Corinthians 10:4 (ESV)

Reflection: Ask the Lord for a sense of His living water flowing through you today.

Prayer: *Thank You Lord, for "that day" which you have planned. I long to walk in Your light and let Your river flow over me eternally. Help me to have patience in the meantime.*

105

"Then those who feared Yahweh talked to one another about this, and Yahweh took note and listened; and a book of remembrance was written in His presence recording those who feared Him and kept His name in mind. 17.'On the day when I act, says Yahweh Sabaoth, they will be my most prized possession, and I shall spare them in the way a man spares the son who serves Him." Malachi 3:16-17 (NJB)

Do you know that your name is written in God's book of remembrance? Most Biblical versions use the word, "remembrance," when translating this verse. The Merriam Webster dictionary defines remembrance as the state of bearing in mind, or something that serves to keep in mind. God always has you on His mind. You are His precious daughter. He keeps a record of your faithfulness to Him. That record does not include your sins or failures. The Bible tells us that as far as the east is from the west, that's how far He has removed all of your mistakes from you.

Do you believe that you are His most prized possession? Other translations say that we are His special treasure. Treasures or prized possessions usually have either high monetary or sentimental value. We don't hold monetary value in ourselves, but we are still His most prized possessions. The new and old King James versions says that He "makes us His jewels." We are the rubies, diamonds, sapphires and emeralds of His crown. There is nothing of higher value to Him.

She is Free Indeed

But there is also no one He values higher or lower than another. You may look at pastors and missionaries, authors and speakers and find yourself lacking in comparison. That is a lie. Each of God's children is equally precious in His sight.

"All who are victorious will be clothed in white. I will never erase their names from the Book of Life, but I will announce before my Father and His angels that they are mine." Revelation 3:5 (NLT)

Reflection: How is God revealing to you that you are His special treasure?

Prayer: *Thank You, Lord that I can find my worth in You. Thank You for including me in Your family, for making me a beautiful jewel in your crown. Let my life reflect Your glory.*

106

"'For look, the Day is coming, glowing like a furnace. All the proud and all the evil-doers will be the stubble, and the Day, when it comes, will set them ablaze, says Yahweh Sabaoth, leaving them neither root nor branch. 20.But for you who fear my name, the Sun of justice will rise with healing in His rays, and you will come out leaping like calves from the stall, 21.and trample on the wicked, who will be like ashes under the soles of your feet on the day when I act, says Yahweh Sabaoth." Malachi 3:19-21 (NJB)

What a contrast between the judgment for the unrighteous and the reward for the righteous. God is light. Light exposes everything. The Son of justice will rise, illuminating those who have trusted in God and in the righteousness of Christ. You will receive your long-awaited justice. Your joy will be like the joy of a young animal. If you have ever seen baby farm animals; new born calves, lambs, and goats joyfully leap about with abandon. Their little dances are adorable and quite hilarious. They simply enjoy life!

What a picture to imagine dancing on the ashes of the wicked. That freedom can only come when the wicked are no more. In that day, there will be no one left to accuse you, no one left to speak harshly to you, no one left who could lay a hand on you, no one left to harass you. You will be utterly, completely free!

If you fear His name, if you love Him and follow Him and accept His forgiveness and His righteousness, this will indeed be you someday. Your God is coming. He is near. Reach out to Him today in the hope of what your future will look like.

*"The Lord has removed your punishment; he
has turned back your enemy.
The King of Israel, the Lord, is among you;
you need no longer fear harm."*
Zephaniah 3:15 (CSB)

Reflection: Are you able to rejoice now about what will one day be?

Prayer: *Lord I long for the day that I will dance and skip about like a baby animal without a care. Thank You that Your Son of Righteousness is on the way, and that You will give me total justice.*

❊ 107 ❊

"The word of Yahweh came to me, saying: 5.'Before I formed you in the womb I knew you; before you came to birth I consecrated you; I appointed you as prophet to the nations.' 6.I then said, 'Ah, ah, ah, Lord Yahweh; you see, I do not know how to speak: I am only a child!' 7.But Yahweh replied, 'Do not say, "I am only a child," for you must go to all to whom I send you and say whatever I command you. 8.Do not be afraid of confronting them, for I am with you to rescue you, Yahweh declares.' 9.Then Yahweh stretched out His hand and touched my mouth, and Yahweh said to me: 'There! I have put my words into your mouth."Jeremiah 1:4-9 (NJB)

God was calling Jeremiah to be one of His prophets during a critical time in Israel's history. Jeremiah prophesied during the years of King Josiah, the last God-fearing King of Judah, and into the captivity of Judah by Babylon. Like Moses and others before Him, Jeremiah insisted that he could not do this, that he did not have what it was going to take to be God's prophet. 1 Corinthians 1:27 (NIV) reads, "But God chose the foolish things of the world to shame the wise; God chose the weak things of the world to shame the strong." Who is a better testament of the power of God than someone who has no strength on his or her own?

What does it mean to you to know that God has had a plan for you even before you were born? He has a calling for you!

You may feel weak, you may feel unqualified or unworthy. That is actually good news. It means that you are in the right condition to be used by God. When you have nothing to give, it gives Him the opportunity to give you everything. When you are empty, He fills you up. And then whatever you accomplish goes to His glory alone.

"But he said to me, "My grace is sufficient for you, for my power is made perfect in weakness. Therefore, I will boast all the more gladly about my weaknesses, so that Christ's power may rest on me."
2 Corinthians 12:9 (NIV)

Reflection: Does it give you peace to know that the Lord has a plan for you?

Prayer: *Thank You, Lord, that Your hand has been upon me even before I was born. Thank You that You have a plan for my life. Help me to trust You and offer myself up to be used for Your glory.*

❈ 108 ❈

"Yahweh says this, 'Let the sage not boast of wisdom, nor the valiant of valour, nor the wealthy of riches! 23.But let anyone who wants to boast, boast of this: of understanding and knowing me. For I amYahweh, who acts with faithful love, justice, and uprightness on earth; yes, these are what please me,' Yahweh declares." Jeremiah 9:22-23 (NJB)

In the last devotional we talked about God working through our weakness with His strength. These verses are a warning. They are a warning to remember that the source of any wisdom, strength or resources is not us. It is God who provides all of these things for us.

There are many flashy preachers and teachers out there, many of whom have gotten rich off of the gospel. But the Lord favors those who humbly recognize their own failings and acknowledge that any good thing in them comes from Jesus. What are we to boast about? Understanding and knowing the Lord. And if we truly understand and know the Lord, our boast will naturally be of Him and His power and His glory. Psalm 34:2 (NASB) reads, "My soul will make its boast in the Lord; The humble will hear it and rejoice."

Where do faithful love, justice and righteousness come from? They come from the Lord. When you feel full of love or see others acting in selfless love, acknowledge the source-give glory to the Lord. When you see justice won for the oppressed-give praise to the God of justice. When you walk in uprightness, remember that it is Christ's righteousness that you are clothed in, and that your own deeds are worthless without Him.

So then, as the scripture says, "Whoever wants to boast must boast of what the Lord has done." I Corinthians 1:31 (GNT)

Reflection: As you look back on your life, where do you see God's strength at work?

Prayer: *Thank You, Lord, that You are the source of all love, all justice, all strength and all righteousness. Help me never to forget that everything I have comes from You. Help me to remember to always give glory to You.*

❋ 109 ❋

"Yahweh, there is no one like you, so great you are, so great your mighty name. 7. Who would not revere you, King of nations? Yes, this is your due. Since of all the wise among the nations, and in all their kingdoms, there is not a single one like you... By His power he made the earth, by His wisdom set the world firm, but His discernment spread out the Heavens. 13. When he thunders there is a roaring of waters in Heaven; he raises clouds from the remotest parts of the earth, makes the lightning flash for the downpour, and brings the wind from His storehouse." Jeremiah 10:6-7, 12-13 (NJB)

Jeremiah is referred to as the weeping prophet. He did not enjoy His calling. He often got upset with God. But there are many moments where he stops and remembers who God is, and that He is worthy of praise. Who is a god like our God? Who created the Heavens and the earth? Our God. Who created our atmosphere and weather systems? Our God. His original design was perfect. Unfortunately, sin entered the world and corrupted His design. But still He demonstrates His power again and again. He set you free, didn't He? Just as He delivered His people Israel over and over again.

We must acknowledge His greatness. We must revere the King of kings and the Lord of lords. Praise is indeed due to Him, our creator. While He has done great and mighty things for humankind, He is also in the little things. Take time today to remember what the Lord has done for you. Praise Him for the big things and for the small things. Praise Him for everything that puts a smile on your face today. Praise Him for always being with you and providing for your needs.

*"Praise the Lord.
Praise God in His sanctuary;
praise Him in His mighty Heavens.
Praise Him for His acts of power; praise
Him for His surpassing greatness." Psalm
150:1-2 (NIV)*

Reflection: Write out your praises to the Lord today.

Prayer: *Praise you, Lord, for all that You have done, all that You do and all that You will do for me. I give You glory for every victory and every good thing, great and small in my life.*

110

"When your words came, I devoured them: your word was my delight and the joy of my heart; for I was called by your Name Yahweh, God Sabaoth."
Jeremiah 15:16 (NJB)

Yahweh Saboath is translated, "Lord of the hosts." This name of God represents His sovereignty over the spiritual and physical worlds and His total and complete victory. It is interesting that Jeremiah chose to use that name in this passage. Most translations refer to actually eating the word. You often hear people commenting on a baby or a little one, "Oh, I could just eat you up!" What provokes such a response? It is an overwhelming sense of how incredible, how beautiful and how wonderful something is, and there are no other words to describe the feeling. Jeremiah was ready to devour those words because he recognized who was speaking them. The Lord of hosts, the God of all victories was humbling Himself to give His words to a simple human. How overwhelming that must have felt. While Jeremiah did not necessarily appreciate everything the Lord instructed him to say, he knew in his heart that these words would sustain him, that they would nourish him when he had nothing else. Though the words were often hard, Jeremiah still felt joy in his heart and was delighted that God chose to speak to him.

She is Free Indeed

We are blessed to have the Bible, the words of God. There are millions of people around the world who do not have access to God's word in the form of the Bible. Be thankful today for the blessing of being able to devour His words.

"My son, pay attention to what I say; turn your ear to my words. Do not let them out of your sight, keep them within your heart; for they are life to those who find them and health to one's whole body." Proverbs 4:20-22 (NIV)

Reflection: What are some of your favorite passages of Scripture?

Prayer: *Thank You, Lord, that You are sovereign and that You hold victory in your hands. Help me to delight in Your words today.*

111

"Yahweh says this, 'Accursed be anyone who trusts in human beings, who relies on human strength and whose heart turns from Yahweh. 6.Such a person is like scrub in the wastelands: when good comes, it does not affect Him since he lives in the parched places of the desert, uninhabited, salt land. 7. Blessed is anyone who trusts in Yahweh, with Yahweh to rely on. 8.Such a person is like a tree by the waterside that thrusts its roots to the stream: when the heat comes it has nothing to fear, its foliage stays green; untroubled in a year of drought, it never stops bearing fruit." Jeremiah 17:5-8 (NJB)

What a contrast between those who trust in God and those who don't. Those who trust in God are blessed. In Biblical terms, being blessed means to be made holy, and to be set apart for God. We are blessed because we can rely on God. Someone who can be relied upon is trustworthy. We humans can only be trustworthy to a point. We all fail. But the Lord is always trustworthy.

Those who trust in the Lord are compared to a tree planted beside water. Trees close to water grow strong and are well nourished. Trees planted along a water source also contribute to the stability of the banks. The roots grow down and make those banks strong. When drought comes along, that tree does not die because it is still close to the water source and has grown roots deeply enough that it finds sustenance under the ground. And these trees are always bearing fruit.

She is Free Indeed

What is the person like who trusts in the Lord, the only One who can always be relied upon? They are strong, full of life, blessed, healthy, and fruit bearing. Doesn't that sound wonderful? Put your whole trust in the Lord today.

"They are like trees planted along the riverbank, bearing fruit each season. Their leaves never wither, and they prosper in all they do."
Psalm 1:3 (NLT)

Reflection: Using the tree analogy, what does your spiritual life look like right now?

Prayer: *Lord, help me to know that I can fully trust, and fully lean on You. Thank You that You will nourish and sustain my soul as I put myself under your care.*

112

" I am a laughing-stock all day long, they all make fun of me… But Yahweh is at my side like a mighty hero; my opponents will stumble, vanquished, confounded by their failure; everlasting, unforgettable disgrace will be theirs.
12. Yahweh Sabaoth, you who test the upright, observer of motives and thoughts, I shall see your vengeance on them, for I have revealed my cause to you. 13. Sing to Yahweh, praise Yahweh, for he has delivered the soul of one in need from the clutches of evil doers." Jeremiah 20:7,b11-13 (NJB)

In verses 7-18 of this chapter, Jeremiah pours out his frustrations to the Lord. Jeremiah was surrounded by people who mocked, ridiculed and threatened him with violence. His life was constantly at risk. In this passage he actually curses the day that he was born. But these complaints are interspersed with the truths of who God is and what He has promised to do.

You may feel surrounded by those who don't believe your story. They may accuse you of lying, of being crazy or of betraying Christian principles. You may be facing harsh affidavits or legal letters. But the Lord knows who you really are. He stands by your side as a mighty hero. He alone knows what is in your heart. One day you will indeed see your opponents stumble and fall. You will receive justice.

Notice in verse 13, that Jeremiah praises the Lord for delivering his soul from evil doers. But the irony here is that he had not yet actually been delivered. He was praising God for what he knew God was going to do. The song, "Raise a Hallelujah,"[1] has a line that goes, "I will praise before my breakthrough."

So praise the Lord today for what He has promised He is going to do for you.

"But I know there is someone in Heaven who will come at last to my defense." Job 19:25 (GNT)

Reflection: What is something you know will happen in the future that you can praise the Lord for today?

Prayer: *Lord, I praise You that I will stand with You on the last day and see justice. Thank You that You will totally vindicate me and that I will forever be free from accusers.*

---

1. *(Bethel Music, Jonathan David Helser, Melissa Helser)*

❊ 113 ❊

"Yes, I know what plans I have in mind for you, Yahweh declares, plans for peace, not for disaster, to give you a future and a hope. 12. When you call to me and come and pray to me, I shall listen to you. 13. When you search for me, you will find me; when you search wholeheartedly for me," Jeremiah 29:11-13 (NJB)

Jeremiah 29:11 is one of the most popular verses in the Bible. If you have been around the church for long, you have probably heard it quoted many times. The problem with this verse is that it is often taken out of context. These words were meant for the people of Israel who had been exiled to Babylon. That does not mean we cannot proclaim them over our lives, but it is important to know what these verses actually mean. They are not saying that we will have earthly riches. They are not saying that our troubles are over. Many translations say that the Lord has plans to, "prosper you." But the original Hebrew word here is actually *shalom*, which primarily means peace and well being. There is no promise of physical wealth here, it is about wealth of the soul.

When we call on the Lord, we can access that peace and well being that brings us hope. When we search for Him with all of our hearts, He reveals Himself to us. While knowing that our earthly futures will not be trouble free, He wants us to know that He wants good things for our lives. He has plans for us that include a future for us that is full of hope.

She is Free Indeed

*"Trust in the Lord with all your heart
and lean not on your own understanding;
in all your ways submit to Him,
and he will make your paths straight."*
Proverbs 3:5-6 (NIV)

Reflection: What area of your life do you need *shalom* for today?

Prayer: *Thank You Lord for the hope that is in my future. Help me to seek You with all of my heart so that I can know what Your will is for me. Thank You for promising to be with me in hard times. Thank You for always being trustworthy.*

114

"That day, Yahweh Sabaoth declares, I shall break the yoke now on your neck and snap your chains; and foreigners will enslave you no more, ...For I shall restore you to health and heal your wounds, Yahweh declares, you who used to be called 'Outcast', 'Zion for whom no one cares'." Jeremiah 30:8, 17 (NJB)

The rest of this chapter continues with God's promises of restoration for His people. When He calls them, "Zion," he is referring to the whole na-tion, which had split between Israel and Judah af ter the reign of King Solomon. When the Lord allowed His people to follow their own way, and when they turned their backs on Him, they gave up His protec-tion. Other nations assumed that the God of Israel either didn't exist or had abandoned His people.

During your relationship, your partner treated you as an outcast and he certainly didn't care for you. You may have felt split down the middle, a part of you that felt love for him and a part of you that hated him. But then, Yahweh Saboath, the Lord of hosts, heard your cry and declared freedom over you when He broke the chains of your abusive relationship. He released you from slavery. And now He wants to restore your broken pieces to wholeness and heal your wounds. He wants to change your name to, "Beloved of the Lord."

She is Free Indeed

How are those wounds healed? By simply spending time with Yahweh Rapha, the Lord your healer. Healing comes through reading His word, prayer, worship and communion with Him.

"He sent out His word and healed them, and delivered them from their destruction." Psalm 107:20 (ESV)

Reflection: It is worthwhile to record some of the "little," ways the Lord is bringing healing to your soul. Those things will one day come together as complete healing for you.

Prayer: *Thank You Lord, for making me whole again. Thank You that You never abandon me. Bring healing to my soul as I seek You today.*

115

"Yahweh has appeared to me from afar; I have loved you with an everlasting love and so I still maintain my faithful love for you. 4.I shall build you once more, yes, you will be rebuilt, Virgin of Israel! Once more in your best attire, and with your tambourines, you will go out dancing gaily."
Jeremiah 31:3-4 (NJB)

One of the reasons I love the prophets is that prophecy often involves eloquent poetry and powerful imagery. How does it feel to know that God has loved you with an everlasting love? "Everlasting" in this verse is the Hebrew word, *olam*, which speaks of the past, present and future. It means that God has always loved you, even before you were conceived, and He always will love you. And He wants to rebuild you as He heals your wounds. He sees you dressed beautifully, dancing with a tambourine. A tambourine is not a quiet or soulful instrument. It's a loud, percussion instrument. You wouldn't play a tambourine at a funeral; but you would definitely play one at a wedding or other joyful occasion. Regarding, "dancing gaily," other versions say, "going forth with the dance of the merrymakers." This is obviously a glorious, joy-filled dance.

Right now, this all might seem impossible. You may feel like you have absolutely nothing to celebrate. You need to know that the Lord is working in you and for you to bring you to this place of simple joy and freedom in Him. It is possible. It is coming.

She is Free Indeed

*"You turned my wailing into dancing;
you removed my sackcloth and clothed me with joy,
that my heart may sing your praises and not be silent.
Lord my God, I will praise you forever."*
Psalm 30:11-12 (NIV)

Reflection: Dancing with a tambourine might seem daunting. What is a less dramatic way that you could show your gratefulness to the Lord today?

Prayer: *Lord, I Thank You that Your love for me is everlasting. I long for the day when I can dance and rejoice before You. Give me hope that this day is coming.*

❋ 116 ❋

"Ah, Lord Yahweh, you made the Heavens and the earth by your great power and outstretched arm. To you nothing is impossible." Jeremiah 32:17 (NJB)

Can you imagine the great power of the Most High God? How incredible is it that He created the universe with its complex systems, and yet took the time to beautifully craft the intricate details of every flower?

You may remember Michelangelo's painting, The Creation of Adam, depicting God's arm stretched from Heaven to earth to reach toward Adam. Who do we reach out our arms to? Mostly, the people we love. Know that God always has His arms outstretched, waiting for you to run into them. He longs to hold and comfort you.

Nothing is impossible with God. He can do anything. So bring Him all of your impossibles today. Bring Him your health impossibles, bring Him your legal impossibles, bring Him your family impossibles, bring Him your financial impossibles, bring Him your relationship impossibles. Lay them all down on His altar and ask Him do to the impossible for you. When you have put everything before Him, stand back and watch Him work. And if it ends up not looking like what you pictured or hoped for, know that he is doing

She is Free Indeed

something else, something better, something that will bring glory to Him.

"But Jesus looked at them and said, "With man this is impossible, but with God all things are possible." Matthew 19:26 (ESV)

Reflection: Write a list of the impossible things in your life. Do you trust the Lord with them?

Prayer: *Lord I bring to you my list of impossibles. Help me to have faith that You will work in all of these areas. Help me to have patience while I wait. Help me not to lose sight if things take longer than I think they should.*

❋ 117 ❋

"While Jeremiah was confined in the Court of the Guard, the word of Yahweh came to Him as follows, 16.'Go and say to Ebed-Melech the Cushite, "Yahweh, God of Israel says this: Look, I am about to perform my words about this city for its ruin and not for its prosperity. That day they will come true before your eyes. 17.But I shall rescue you that day, Yahweh declares, and you will not be handed over to the hands of the men you fear. 18.Yes, I shall certainly rescue you: you will not fall to the sword; you will escape with your life, because you have put your trust in me, Yahweh declares." Jeremiah 39:15-18 (NJB)

Ebed-Melech was a Cushite (African) slave at Zedekiah's palace. When he heard that Jeremiah had been thrown into the pit, he begged the king for clemency and was given permission to help pull Jeremiah out of the pit. It is interesting that in the middle of dire prophecies of judgment on the whole nations of Judah and Israel, God takes the time to show mercy to one man, a slave, a eunuch, someone in no way related to God's chosen people and someone not valued in that time and place. A eunuch would not have even been allowed in the Hebrew temple.

This passage demonstrates that the God of the universe loves every single one of His children. There are none He overlooks. He recognized Ebed-Melech's trust in Him and He richly rewarded him by promising to protect him from the coming calamity.

Do you ever feel like the Lord overlooks you? Do you feel like He has forgotten you? He hasn't. He sees your trust in Him and He will reward it. Have you drifted away from communion with Him lately and now feel ashamed? There is nothing to worry about. The Lord is right there in front of you with open arms waiting to take you back in His arms.

"Suppose one of you has a hundred sheep and loses one of them. Doesn't he leave the ninety-nine in the open country and go after the lost sheep until he finds it?" Luke 15:4 (NIV)

Reflection: What lies have you been told that stop you from believing how special you are to the Lord?

Prayer: *Thank You, Lord, that You see me and You love me. Thank You that nothing will ever stop Your faithfulness to me. Thank You that You always have time for me.*

118

"Then all the military leaders, in particular Johanan son of Kareah and Azariah son of Hoshaiah, and all the people from least to greatest, approached 2.the prophet Jeremiah and said, 'Please hear our petition and intercede with Yahweh your God for us and for all this remnant -- and how few of us are left out of many, your own eyes can see- 3.so that Yahweh your God may show us the way we are to go and what we must do.' 4. The prophet Jeremiah replied, 'I hear you; I will indeed pray to Yahweh your God as you ask; and whatever answer Yahweh your God gives you, I will tell you, keeping nothing back from you.'...7. Ten days later the word of Yahweh came to Jeremiah." Jeremiah 42:1-4, 7 (NJB)

There are two remarkable things about this passage. The first is that the military leaders who were left in Judah wanted to flee the Babylonians and head back to Egypt. After all that they had been through, they somehow thought going back to slavery in Egypt was the best option. There may be times that you want to go back to that destructive relationship. It may feel like it would be safer there, because it's familiar, because you know what to expect. Going back into slavery is never the right answer. Unfortunately, the military leaders did not listen to the word of the Lord. They fled back to Egypt and eventually the Babylonians invaded Egypt as well.

The other interesting point is that the Lord did not answer Jeremiah for 10 whole days. I imagine those were long, uncomfortable days both for Jeremiah and the military leaders. We aren't told why God took so long in answering. Jeremiah had a direct line to Heaven as one of God's prophets. Did Jeremiah start to doubt Himself or His calling? Did the leaders think that God had completely abandoned them? We don't know, but we do know ourselves what it feels like to wait for the Lord. It is incredible hard, incredibly uncomfortable. But the Lord was faithful, He did answer. And He will answer you when the time is right.

"I wait for the LORD, my whole being waits, and in His word I put my hope." Psalm 130:5 (NIV)

Reflection: What are you waiting on the Lord for today?

> **Prayer:** *Lord help me never to run back to Egypt. Help me to never enter another destructive relationship. When I have questions, give me patience as I wait for Your perfect word with Your perfect will.*

❈ 119 ❈

"'And I said to you, "Do not take fright, do not be afraid of them. 30. Yah-weh your God goes ahead of you and will be fighting on your side, just as you saw Him act in Egypt. 31. You have seen Him in the desert too: Yahweh your God continued to support you, as a man supports His son, all along the road you followed until you arrived here." 32. But for all this, you put no faith in Yahweh your God, 33. going ahead of you on the journey to find you a camping ground, by night in the fire to light your path, and in the cloud by day." Deuteronomy 1:29-33 (NJB)

In Deuteronomy God is giving final instructions to the people of Israel before they enter the Promised land.

Over and over throughout their long and perilous journey, the Israelites faced what seemed to be insurmountable obstacles. And every time, they doubted the Lord and lost their faith, and every time God met them and took care of their needs. While it is easy to shake our heads at their lack of belief, especially given all of the miracles the Lord had worked on their behalf, we forget how often we, too do the same.

It is so easy to get caught up in the busyness of our post-modern lives. We have so many balls up in the air at any given time. It is so easy to focus on them and lose our focus on Jesus. Where do you go first when you have a problem? Do you call a friend or family member? While they often have valuable advice, Jesus wants us to come to Him first.

She is Free Indeed

The Lord goes before you, He fights beside you. He supports and leads you. He is there by day and he is there by night. He never ceases watching over you.

"You know when I sit and when I rise; you perceive my thoughts from afar.
You discern my going out and my lying down; you are familiar with all my ways." Psalm 139:2-3 (NIV)

Reflection: Think about the troubles you are facing today. Have you brought them before the Lord?

Prayer: *Thank You, Lord, that You have always been at my side, You have never left me alone. Help me to remember to come to You first with my needs. Help me to never forget everything You have done for me.*

❋ 120 ❋

"Look: as Yahweh my God commanded me, I have taught you laws and customs, for you to observe in the country of which you are going to take possession. 6.Keep them, put them into practice, and other peoples will admire your wisdom and prudence. Once they know what all these laws are, they will exclaim, "No other people is as wise and prudent as this great nation!" 7. And indeed, what great nation has its gods as near as Yahweh our God is to us whenever we call to Him? 8.And what great nation has laws and customs as upright as the entirety of this Law which I am laying down for you today?" Deuteronomy 4:5-8 (NJB)

While we as Christians are no longer under the law, we still do our best to uphold it. When we endeavor to honor the Lord in our daily lives, we are an example to others. While many Christians who don't have a full understanding of the Biblical marriage covenant may feel that you disobeyed the Lord by leaving your marriage; by your living an upright life (to the best of your ability) with Jesus by your side, they will soon have little to criticize.

But the most important thing is the way we appear to people who do not know Jesus. When we are walking in fellowship with Jesus, it should be obvious to others that there is something different about us. Our actions and reactions are different. They are full of grace.

That's not to say you will not fail. You will. We all will. But when we do, we bring our failure before the cross and we exchange our sin for Jesus' righteousness. If we have failed another person, we go to them with a sincere apology.

At the end of the day, you stand before Christ alone. He sees and knows your heart. Don't let anyone condemn you.

"Consider the blameless, observe the upright; a future awaits those who seek peace." Psalm 37:37 (NIV)

Reflection: When we face difficult times in our lives, our true character often shows itself. What would others say about your character?

Prayer: *Lord help me to demonstrate character and integrity in all that I do. Show me when I am wrong so that I might quickly correct it. I ask that others would see You in me.*

121

"But take care, as you value your lives! Do not forget the things which you yourselves have seen, or let them slip from your heart as long as you live; teach them, rather, to your children and to your children's children."
Deuteronomy 4:9 (NJB)

This is another reminder to remember and reflect on the goodness of God and all that He has done for you. Take time daily to make a list of the things you are thankful for. In recent years the research around gratitude has exploded. Gratitude actually changes your brain. As you practice it more and more, new neural pathways form in your brain and change it so that your first impulse is to be thankful rather than to complain. It takes work, though. Make it a daily habit. A gratitude journal is a great way to start. Start by writing down a few items daily and then challenge yourself to write more and more each day.

And talk to others about the things God has done for you. Sharing your testimony is a powerful thing. It can bless and encourage others. It is also vital to share the good things the Lord has done with you with your children (if you have children) on a regular basis. Children's brains are most profoundly influenced by their parents. So teach your children about the faithfulness of the Lord and remind them over and over of the miracles the Lord has worked for you.

She is Free Indeed

"Give thanks to the LORD, for he is good. His love endures forever."
Psalm 136:1 (NIV)

Reflection: List 10 things you are thankful for today.

Prayer: *Thank You, Lord for everything You have done for me. Help me never to forget about Your faithfulness. Give me opportunities to share my story with others so that they may be encouraged.*

122

"Put this question, then, to the ages that are past, that have gone before you, from when God created the human race on earth: Was there ever a word so majestic, from one end of Heaven to the other? Was anything like it ever heard? 33. Did ever a people hear the voice of the living God speaking from the heart of the fire, as you have heard it, and remain alive? 34. Has it ever been known before that any god took action Himself to bring one nation out of another one, by ordeals, signs, wonders, war with mighty hand and outstretched arm, by fearsome terrors -- all of which things Yahweh your God has done for you before your eyes in Egypt? 35. 'This he showed you, so that you might know that Yahweh is the true God and that there is no other."
Deuteronomy 4:32-35 (NJB)

In ancient times the peoples served many gods. In that time religion was mostly about trying to appease the gods and avoid punishment. There was no thought of a benevolent, loving God.

The Most High God had performed incredible miracles for His people. And this was even before the cross. The Lord had led them out of Egypt, He had parted the Red Sea so that they could walk right through it, He had brought them water out of rocks and food that fell from the sky. He had routed every enemy before them and was about to lead them into the Promised Land. But every step of the way the Israelites grumbled, complained and lost their faith. They took their eyes off of their provider and put them on their problems.

She is Free Indeed

We all fall into this trap. We need to keep reminding ourselves that God has brought us out of Egypt, 'by ordeals, signs, wonders, and war." He stretched out that awesome arm, His mighty hand worked wonders.

Who is a God like our God? If you compare contemporary religions you will find no other god who speaks to His people, who performs miracles for His people, who is a God of love who pours grace and mercy out on His people.

"Who is like You among the gods, O Lord? Who is like You, majestic in holiness, Awesome in praises, working wonders?"
Exodus 15:11 (NIV)

Reflection: Make a list of the miraculous things the Lord has done for you.

Prayer: *I am so thankful that I serve the Most High God, maker of Heaven and earth. Thank You for pouring out love on your people. Thank You for working miracles for me. Keep my eyes fixed on You today, Jesus.*

❋ 123 ❋

"Honour your father and your mother, as Yahweh your God has commanded you, so that you may have long life and may prosper in the country which Yahweh your God is giving you." Deuteronomy 5:16 (NJB)

This may be one of the most difficult commandments for you. Many who went into abusive romantic relationships came from abusive families. How are you then expected to "honor," those who abused you? The word, "honor," in this passage is the Hebrew word, *kabad*. It means to be heavy, weighty or burdensome. I believe it means that we need to take seriously the roles our parents played. We can't do anything to change our heritage. We carry their DNA no matter how awful that makes us feel.

So how do we honor? The answer lies in what the opposite of honoring looks like.

Rather than curse, bless and pray for them.

Rather than fight, make peace-which may mean that you need to set up some strong boundaries in order to keep yourself safe.

Rather than complain about them, try to remember some of the good that they did.

She is Free Indeed

This is the only commandment with a promise attached to it. Apparently respecting your parents is important enough that God links it to your health and prosperity. You can honor someone while still protecting yourself from him or her. If you have a particularly toxic parent, the safest thing you might consider that honors them is to send a card or note in the mail on holidays. In that way, you are protecting your boundaries while still showing respect to them.

"Every one of you shall revere His mother and His father, and you shall keep my Sabbaths: I am the Lord your God." Leviticus 19:3 (ESV)

Reflection: Try to think of some good memories of your parents. Are you able to be grateful for them?

Prayer: *Lord, I Thank You that You are my perfect Father. Thank You that You meet the needs in my life that my parents did not. Help me to create healthy boundaries while at the same time continuing to honor my parents.*

124

"Listen, Israel: Yahweh our God is the one, the only Yahweh. 5. You must love Yahweh your God with all your heart, with all your soul, with all your strength. 6. Let the words I enjoin on you today stay in your heart. 7. You shall tell them to your children, and keep on telling them, when you are sitting at home, when you are out and about, when you are lying down and when you are standing up; 8. you must fasten them on your hand as a sign and on your forehead as a headband; 9. you must write them on the doorposts of your house and on your gates." Deuteronomy 6:4-9 (NJB)

What does it mean to love the Lord with all your heart? The word used in Hebrew is, *lebab*, which refers to the inner person, mind, will and heart. It means that everything within you loves everything about Him. What does it mean to love the Lord with all your soul? The Hebrew word, *nephesh*, refers to your life, your self, your appetites, desires and emotions. What does is mean to love the Lord with all your strength? The Hebrew world for strength here is, *meod*, which means muchness, force and abundance. This word is used in other passages of Scripture where it is translated, "very much," or "greatly." We could use the word, "passionately." There is a force behind passion. There is energy in passion. Passion is obvious to others. The Lord wants to encounter you in your mind, body and spirit. He wants all of you devoted to all of Him.

The rest of this passage talks about keeping the Lord and His word constantly in mind and regularly talking about His love with others. You may write down your favorite verses and put them on your mirror, or you may have Scripture-based art around your home. The point is to stay close to the Lord at all times and to teach others about Him.

"Jesus replied: 'Love the Lord your God with all your heart and with all your soul and with all your mind. This is the first and greatest command -ment.'" Matthew 22:37-38 (NIV)

Reflection: What do you think your life would look life if you loved the Lord with absolutely everything in you?

Prayer: *Lord, help me to passionately love You with all of my inner soul, my mind, my heart my will, my desires, my mind. Help me to keep You always on my heart and in my mind.*

125

"When Yahweh has brought you into the country which he swore to your ancestors Abraham, Isaac and Jacob that he would give you, with great and prosperous cities you have not built, with houses full of good things you have not provided, with wells you have not dug, with vineyards and olive trees you have not planted, and then, when you have eaten as much as you want, be careful you do not forget Yahweh who has brought you out of Egypt, out of the place of slave-labour. Yahweh your God is the one you must fear, Him alone you must serve, His is the name by which you must swear."
Deuteronomy 6:10-13 (NJB)

Though it might be hard to imagine right now, at some point your life will settle down and things will begin to go better for you. It is so easy during those times to forget our dependence on the Lord. When our needs become less, we pray less. When our emotions settle down, we call on Him less. When we feel better, we invariably take on more and have less time for the Lord. This is why it is important to set time aside during the day for the Lord. It may be that you read your Bible after breakfast, or you do a family devotional after supper. You may get up 15 minutes early to pray or pray before you go to bed. Once you have developed a habit, it becomes easier and easier.

Practicing gratitude is another way to keep yourself from forgetting Who it is who set you free and has blessed you. When you willfully recognize each day that all good things come from the Father, you remember your dependence upon Him. If you have a gratitude journal, from time to time go back and read over your entries from the past to remember what the Lord has done for you.

"Every good and perfect gift is from above, coming down from the Father of the Heavenly lights, who does not change like shifting shadows."
James 1:17 (NIV)

Reflection: Pick a time that works for you most days, and put an appointment with the Lord on your calendar.

Prayer: *Thank You, Lord for all of the good things You have done for me and for all that You have blessed me with. I give You praise today.*

126

"For you are a people consecrated to Yahweh your God; of all the peoples on earth, you have been chosen by Yahweh your God to be His own people. 7. Yahweh set His heart on you and chose you not because you were the most numerous of all peoples -- for indeed you were the smallest of all- 8. but because he loved you and meant to keep the oath which he swore to your ancestors: that was why Yahweh brought you out with His mighty hand and redeemed you from the place of slave-labour, from the power of Pharaoh king of Egypt." Deuteronomy 7:6-8 (NJB)

While this passage refers to the people of Israel, we, as followers of Jesus, have also been adopted into the family of God. How does it feel to know that you, specifically you, were chosen by God? Why did He choose you? It wasn't because of your strength or your intelligence or your abilities. He chose you because He loves you. It's that simple. He loves you. And because He loves you! He set you free from that destructive relationship. He redeemed you, He bought you back.

God has set His seal upon you. You are His. Other versions say that we are a, "holy people," and, "a special treasure." So don't let anyone else affix a label to you. You are not crazy, you are not deranged, you are not a liar, you are not a backslider, you are not disobeying God by leaving the relationship, you are not weak, you are not pathetic. And while you may indeed feel like a victim now, the Lord is going to make you a survivor because you are His and He has won the victory for you. So walk with your head held high. You are the treasure of the Almighty.

"Now it is God who makes both us and you stand firm in Christ. He anointed us, set His seal of ownership on us, and put His Spirit in our hearts as a deposit, guaranteeing what is to come."
2 Corinthians 1:21-22 (NIV)

Reflection: Spend some time thinking about who God is. Then ruminate on the fact that the Almighty God chose you.

Prayer: *Thank You Lord, for choosing me and setting me free. Thank You for loving me for who I am. Thank You that You have a plan for me that is good. Help me to keep my eyes fixed on You. I love You, Jesus.*

❊ 127 ❊

"'Listen to these ordinances, be true to them and observe them, and in return Yahweh your God will be true to the covenant and love which he promised on oath to your ancestors. He will love you and bless you and increase your numbers; he will bless the fruit of your body and the produce of our soil, your corn, your new wine, your oil, the issue of your cattle, the young of our flock, in the country which he swore to your ancestors that he would give you. You will be the most blessed of all peoples. " Deuteronomy 7:12-14a (NJB)

These verses describe God's perfect plan. They demonstrate that only good things come from the Lord. He wants his people to be at peace and to live healthy lives. He does not want us to face sickness and disease, poverty, war, natural disasters or abuse. Too often these things are blamed on God. Natural disasters are described as, "acts of God." But none of those things are part of His plan for His people.

God created a beautiful, perfect world. His plan was to walk with human beings, side by side in perfect communion. Unfortunately, God has an enemy, Satan. The enemy deceived Adam and Eve into sinning against God. And once sin entered the picture, God's plans were seriously hindered.

So, if God wants good and beautiful things for us, why are there so many problems? One answer is simply the fact that human beings have free will. Most of the trouble in the world is caused simply by our bad decisions and the bad decisions of others. The rest of the problems in the world come from the enemy. Some modern Biblical scholars even believe that "natural" disasters are acts of Satan.

Know that the Lord is for you. He wants good things for you. He wants to bless you. The destructive things in your life do not come from him.

"I would have despaired unless I had believed that
I would see the goodness of the Lord
In the land of the living.
Wait for the Lord;
Be strong and let your heart take courage;
Yes, wait for the Lord." Psalm 27:13-14 (NASB)

Reflection: Think about something that happened in your life that you were angry with God for. How does it feel to know that bad things are not His will and do not come from Him?

Prayer: *Thank You Lord, that You are good and that You want good things for me. I ask for Your blessing in all areas of my life today as I seek You. Help me to remember that You are not the author of destruction, sickness or evil.*

128

"You may say in your heart, "These nations outnumber me; how shall I be able to dispossess them?" Do not be afraid of them: remember how Yahweh your God treated Pharaoh and all Egypt, the great ordeals that you yourselves have seen, the signs and wonders, the mighty hand and outstretched arm with which Yahweh your God brought you out. This is how Yahweh your God will treat all the peoples whom you fear to face."
Deuteronomy 7:17-19 (NJB)

About to enter the Promised Land, the nation of Israel had an army of around 600,000. This tiny army was facing 7 nations. How daunting that must have been! They must have felt completely overwhelmed and inadequate. But the Lord was reminding them again to look back and remember what He had already done for them. He had already accomplished many, many impossible things.. In this journey you will face problems and people much more powerful than you. You will face mountains that seem insurmountable. Remember that the Lord has been with you every step of the way. Every step of their journey, God worked miracles. Over and over He demonstrated His power and His glory.

Where would we be without Jesus? None of us would have made it far. He has always been with us and He always will be. Instead of looking at your problems and the obstacles that lie in your path, look to Jesus. Put the cross in between you and those mountains. Ask the Lord how He is going to help

She is Free Indeed

solve those problems for you. Call to mind those things He has already done. Thank Him for them.

"But Jesus looked at them and said, 'With man this is impossible, but with God all things are possible.'" Matthew 19:26 (ESV)

Reflection: Think about one of the challenges that you face. How could you trust the Lord with it today?

Prayer: *Thank You, Lord, that You are bigger than my problems. Thank You that You have and always will be faithful. I give You my problems today and ask that You do the impossible.*

129

"Do not be afraid of them, for Yahweh your God is among you, a great and terrible God. Little by little, Yahweh your God will clear away these nations before you; you cannot destroy them all at once, or wild animals will breed and be disastrous for you. But Yahweh your God will put them at your mercy, and disaster after disaster will overtake them until they are finally destroyed."
Deuteronomy 7: 21-23 (NJB)

As much as we would love a whirlwind solution to all our problems, that rarely happens. God led his people on a journey out of Egypt. He didn't teleport them from Egypt to an empty glorious paradise. Instead He took them on a journey where they would have to absolutely trust Him the entire time. From the Red Sea to crossing the Jordan, God provided everything they needed. And now, at the pinnacle of their journey He tells them that now they must battle to clear out the promised land for themselves. Again, there was no single perfect battle where all their enemies were destroyed. Instead, "little by little," the Lord worked alongside them to vanquish their enemies.

Journeys are a time of deep learning. If the Lord were to suddenly wipe out all of your problems and concerns and give you absolutely everything you need, what then? You would not have learned to trust Him at every step. You would not need him to do anything more. Would you still seek him as much? Would you have learned anything along the way? Probably not.

She is Free Indeed

The Lord loves to walk with us along our journeys, clearing obstacles away one by one. As we walk with Him in this, we learn great truths and we learn to be completely dependent upon Him.

"And we all, who with unveiled faces contemplate the Lord's glory, are being transformed into his image with ever-increasing glory, which comes from the Lord, who is the Spirit." 2 Corinthians 3:18 (NIV)

Reflection: Think of some of the things you have already learned on this journey. Write them down so that you remember them.

> **Prayer:** *Lord give me patience along this journey. Help me to learn what You want me to learn at each step. Thank You that You promise to be with me.*

130

"Remember the long road by which Yahweh your God led you for forty years in the desert, to humble you, to test you and know your inmost heart -- whether you would keep his commandments or not. He humbled you, he made you feel hunger, he fed you with manna which neither you nor your ancestors had ever known, to make you understand that human beings live not on bread alone but on every word that comes from the mouth of Yahweh. The clothes on your back did not wear out and your feet were not swollen, all those forty years. 'Learn from this that Yahweh your God was training you as a man trains his child, and keep the commandments of Yahweh your God, and so follow his ways and fear him." Deuteronomy 8:2-6 (NJB)

These verses continue the theme of the journey. One of the important things to note was that while the Lord was testing and teaching the Israelites, He was right there beside them. He didn't throw them in the water by themselves to see if they could swim. The journey was probably miserable at times, but God needed to know that His people trusted Him. He wanted wonderful things for them in the promised land, but He needed them to prove that they would depend on Him, that they would not forget Him when things became easier. Sadly, as time went on, the Israelites did not remember the Lord and the things He had done. They did not drive out all of the inhabitants of the Promised Land. They decided it was easier to go with the flow, to not have to fight any longer. And because they did not drive those people out, the people of the 7 nations of Canaan ended up influencing the Israelites to the point that they abandoned the Most High and served false gods.

She is Free Indeed

This is why God does not constantly intervene to make our lives completely problem free. He knows how fickle our hearts are, how quickly we forget Him. He also does not want us to forget that Heaven, with Him, is our true home. He doesn't want us to get too focused on this earth.

"For I, the Lord your God, hold your right hand; it is I who say to you, "Fear not, I am the one who helps you." Isaiah 41:14 (ESV)

Reflection: Are you bringing all of your troubles before the Lord each day?

Prayer: *Lord help me to remember to bring everything to You. Help me to trust in Your faithfulness. Keep me close to You as You guide me on this journey.*

131

"Beware of thinking to yourself, "My own strength and the might of my own hand have given me the power to act like this." Remember Yahweh your God; he was the one who gave you the strength to act effectively like this, thus keeping then, as today, the covenant which he swore to your ancestors."
Deuteronomy 8:17-18 (NJB)

Hindsight is always 20/20. In moments of crisis we are often unable to lift our eyes above the chaos to see what God is doing. But after you have been through a valley, as you begin to summit a mountain again, you can look back on what you went through, and see Jesus. It may not be right away; it may be years before you finally see and understand. But He is there, always working. His faithfulness is eternal-it is for the past, the present and the future.

When you succeed, when you find peace and clarity, it is important to remember the source. It is not your own strength that got you out of your calamity, it was Jesus' strength. It was not your might. It was His. The word "might," or *otsem*, in Hebrew can also mean, "bones." Bones supply structure and stability. God was the one who supplied your structure and your ability to get through. To function a body needs bones as well as muscles, which provide the strength.

Stay away from pride which would tell you that you made it through on your own. That is a lie. Yahweh is your provider.

She is Free Indeed

"The LORD is my strength and my shield; my heart trusts in him, and he helps me. My heart leaps for joy, and with my song I praise him."
Psalm 28:7 (NIV)

Reflection: Look back on your life. Where can you now recognize Jesus working where you did not see it before?

Prayer: *Thank You Lord that You alone are my strength, that You work wonders on my behalf. Help me to keep trusting You.*

❋ 132 ❋

"The elders of Israel all assembled, went back to Samuel at Ramah, and said, 'Look, you are old, and your sons are not following your example. So give us a king to judge us, like the other nations.' Samuel thought that it was wrong of them to say, 'Let us have a king to judge us,' so he prayed to Yahweh. But Yahweh said to Samuel, 'Obey the voice of the people in all that they say to you: it is not you they have rejected but me, not wishing me to reign over them anymore. They are now doing to you exactly what they have done to me since the day I brought them out of Egypt until now, deserting me and serving other gods." 1 Samuel 8:4-8 (NJB)

The Israelites here were deceived into thinking that God was not enough for them. They thought they needed a king to protect them. Samuel tried to persuade them against this, and the Lord gave the Israelites a long list of why having a king rather than Yahweh was a bad idea. Verses 19 and 20 of the same passage read, "The people, however, refused to listen to Samuel. They said, 'No! We are determined to have a king, so that we can be like the other nations, with our own king to rule us and lead us and fight our battles.'" In chapter 12, Samuel calls this a "wicked," thing.

It is so easy, after leaving a harmful relationship to want to jump back into another. We want a protector, a provider, a buffer. We want someone to help us feel safe. These are the roles the Lord wants to play in our lives. No man can give us the protection, love and provision that the Lord provides. So, don't fall into the trap of rushing into a new relationship, especially if you are doing so to meet your needs. God is your first husband. You do not need another. Allow Him to heal you and bring you back before considering a new romantic relationship. Falling into a new relationship quickly can be a trap and will not bring about the healing that you are looking for. That kind of healing cannot be found in another human being.

"But my God shall supply all your need according to his riches in glory by Christ Jesus." Philippians 4:19 (NKJ)

Reflection: Ask the Lord today how He is going to meet all of your needs.

Prayer: *Lord help me to come to you first with all of my needs. Help me not to fall into the trap of rushing into a relationship to have my needs met. Thank You that you can meet all of them.*

133

"For the Lord your God is the God of gods and the Lord of lords, the great, the mighty, and the awesome God who does not show partiality nor take a bribe. He executes justice for the orphan and the widow and shows His love for the alien by giving him food and clothing."
Deuteronomy 10:17-18 (NASB)

What a powerful description of who God is! Your God is the God of all gods, the Lord of all lords. He is over all and above all. And yet He calls himself, "yours." He has humbled himself to be owned by His people. When it says He does not show partiality it means that all are equally precious in His sight. He never prefers one over the other.

There is a juxtaposition in this passage-it describes the incredible nature of God but then describes the lowest of the lowly here on earth-the orphan and the widow. In ancient times orphans and widows were often considered to be unlucky or cursed and often lived in abject poverty. Foreigners were also often treated with suspicion. But God is clearly passionate about justice for all.

Who are the people around you who are poor? Are you working on the Lord's behalf for justice for them? Are there refugees in your community that you could be supporting? Jesus loves all of His children. And if we are to follow Him, we need to take up the causes that He takes up. If He is passionate about the

She is Free Indeed

poor and the disregarded, then we need to be as well. Perhaps God will lead you to other women with similar stories that you can come alongside as they walk their healing journeys.

"Pure and undefiled religion in the sight of our God and Father is this: to visit orphans and widows in their distress, and to keep oneself unstained by the world." James 1:27 (NASB)

Reflection: How could you share God's love with someone today?

Prayer: *Thank You, Lord, that in Your majesty and greatness You don't forget the weakest among us. Show me where You are working in my community so that I can join in and bless You by serving others.*

134

"Let these words of mine remain in your heart and in your soul; fasten them on your hand as a sign and on your forehead as a headband. Teach them to your children, and keep on telling them, when you are sitting at home, when you are out and about, when you are lying down and when you are standing up. Write them on the doorposts of your house and on your gates, so that you and your children may live long in the country which Yahweh swore to your ancestors that he would give them for as long as there is a sky above the earth."
Deuteronomy 11:18-21 (NJB)

Over and over in the book of Deuteronomy the Lord reminds His people of the importance of His words. In Old Testament times, men wore little pouches with the Scriptures on their foreheads. Even today Orthodox Jewish men will wear these pouches, called phylacteries, while in prayer.

How closely do you keep the word of God? How much do you read your Bible or speak of God's principles and promises? It is easy to get distracted and too busy for the word. But what in our life can take precedence over God's word? Is it not one of the most important things? These devotionals are based on the word. There would be nothing to say without scripture. In His word we see His love, His faithfulness, His promises, and His desires for relationship with us. If you want to know God, you need to immerse yourself in His word. His word is life. In it you will find joy, peace and freedom. If you go through the Psalms, you will find a prayer for every possible situation that you face. When you cannot find the words to pray yourself, open up the word and let the Lord guide you in prayer.

*"Your word is a lamp for my feet,
a light on my path." Psalm 119:105 (NIV)*

Reflection: How is reading the Bible a part of your daily routine? How do you find it impacts you? If you don't already spend daily time in the word, how can you plan for it and make it a purposeful part of your day?

Prayer: *Lord, Thank You for the gift of the Bible. Help me to keep Your word close to my heart, lead me as I read it each day.*

135

"For if you faithfully keep and observe all these commandments that I enjoin on you today, loving Yahweh your God, following all his ways and holding fast to him, Yahweh will dispossess all these nations before you, and you will dispossess nations greater and more powerful than yourselves." Deuteronomy 11:22-23 (NJB)

There are interesting words used in this passage. The word for, "keep," in Hebrew is *shamar.* As well as to keep, it means to watch, preserve or guard. It is again a reminder of keeping the word of the Lord close to you. The Hebrew word for "hold fast," is, *dabaq*. It means to cling, to cleave and to keep close. It is the word used in other places in the Bible to describe the closeness of the relationship between a husband and wife. Here is yet another reminder that the Lord wants to take the role of a loving husband to you.

These are strong images of the relationship the Lord wants to have with you. He wants you to protect that relationship. He wants you to stay focused and committed. He wants you to hold onto Him tenaciously. And He promises to hold up His end of the deal. He wants to move on your behalf, He wants to give you His strength. While it might be hard for you to imagine what a healthy marriage looks like, an important part is that the relationship involves equal give and take. But in relationship with the Lord, He is the one doing the majority of the giving. He just asks you to stay close to Him. He is your banner.

"For you have been my help, and in the shadow of your wings I will sing for joy. My soul clings to you; your right hand upholds me." Psalm 63:7-8 (ESV)

Reflection: What holds you back from clinging to the Lord?

Prayer: *Lord, I hold fast to You today. My soul clings to You. Help me to never be distracted from the intimacy of our relationship.*

✻ 136 ✻

"There must, then, be no poor among you. For Yahweh will grant you his blessing in the country which Yahweh your God is giving you to possess as your heritage, only if you pay careful attention to the voice Yahweh your God, by keeping and practising all these commandments which I am enjoining on you today. If Yahweh your God blesses you as he has promised, you will be creditors to many nations but debtors to none; you will rule over many nations and be ruled by none. 'Is there anyone poor among you, one of your brothers, in any town of yours in the country which Yahweh your God is giving you? Do not harden your heart or close your hand against that poor brother of yours but be open handed with him and lend him enough for his needs." Deuteronomy 15:4-8 (NJB)

It would seem that if Christians were doing it right, there would be a significant reduction in the problem of poverty around the world. God's plan was that those who had much would share with those who did not. Many single women struggle financially. You may live paycheck to paycheck. You may need to access social services. But it is important to remember that God is our provider and no need is too great for Him. As we are generous with others, He will be generous with us.

What does it mean to be open handed? It means that we give when we feel prompted, even if it makes no sense financially for us. And it also means that our hands are open to the Lord's blessing.

Being generous is as important as every other command the Lord gives. As He promises to be with

She is Free Indeed

us if we hold fast to Him and obey Him, He promises to provide for us as we provide for the needs of others. If we truly trust Him, generosity will come naturally out of that trust that we have in Him to provide for all of our needs.

If this seems daunting, start small. But then be open to giving more and receiving more.

"Give, and it will be given to you. A good measure, pressed down, shaken together and running over, will be poured into your lap. For with the measure you use, it will be measured to you." Luke 6:38 (NIV)

Reflection: Ask the Lord to show you what He wants you to give today.

Prayer: *Thank You, Lord, for Your generosity with me. Help me to trust You as I become more generous. Show me where and what You want me to give today.*

❋ 137 ❋

"You must not allow a master to imprison a slave who has escaped from him and come to you. Let him make his home with you and yours, wherever he pleases in whichever of your towns he prefers; you must not molest him."
Deuteronomy 23:16-17 (NJB)

This is an interesting passage in the middle of lists of commands and regulations. The Lord is saying here that if a slave from another land runs away to Israel for safety, he or she is to be allowed to stay in Israel and create a home there. They are not to allow the slave's master to come and take him or her back.

Isn't that exactly what you did when you ran away from that destructive relationship? If you attend a church, did they offer you refuge, or did they tell you to go back to the relationship? If they did not offer you refuge, then that church is not a safe place for you. You need to find a place where men and women are equally valued, supported and encouraged. The only person in authority over you is Jesus Christ.

God's will for you was that you would run to a safe place, where you would be believed and loved and cared for. If this did not happen, it broke God's heart. I would encourage you to search for a safe harbour, a church or small group that believes you and will stand up for you.

She is Free Indeed

"The LORD is a refuge for the oppressed, a stronghold in times of trouble." Psalm 9:9 (NIV)

Reflection: Do you have a safe harbour, a community that supports you? What is keeping you from finding one?

Prayer: *Thank You, Lord, that You are my safe harbour. Thank You that You have a safe place in mind for me. Lead me to the church and the people who will love and support me in this time.*

❉ 138 ❉

If you return to Yahweh your God, if with all your heart and with all your soul you obey his voice, you and your children, in everything that I am laying down for you today, then Yahweh your God will bring back your captives, he will have pity on you and gather you back from all the peoples among whom Yahweh your God has scattered you. Should you have been banished to the very sky's end, Yahweh your God will gather you again even from there, will come there to reclaim you and bring you back to the country which belonged to your ancestors, so that you may possess it in your turn, and be made prosper-ous there and more numerous than your ancestors."
Deuteronomy 30:2-5 (NJB)

In Deuteronomy 27-29 the Lord outlines the blessings He will give to the Israelites if they follow Him with all their hearts, and the curses that will come upon them if they do not. He speaks of the inevitability of war and exile if His people turn away from Him. Now, in these verses following, we see the passionate love of the Father for His children. He tells them that even if they turn their backs on Him and seek other gods and deny Him, that if they just turn back to Him, all of those curses will be gone, and the blessings will come back.

Perhaps you have strayed a little. Perhaps in your pain you turned your back on Him. Do not let the enemy convince you that all of the horrible things you endured were somehow God's will for your life. They were not. God is light, love, life and truth. There is no darkness in Him. Turn your eyes back to your Fa-th er today. Stretch out your hands toward Him and let Him come and bless you. It won't all happen at once, but the Lord shows His favor to those who seek Him in spirit and in truth.

"Tear your heart, and not your garments, and turn to Yahweh, your God; for he is gracious and merciful, slow to anger, and abundant in loving kindness, and relents from sending calamity." Joel 2:13 (WEB)

Reflection: Ask the Lord to show you if there is an area in your life that you have shut Him out of.

Prayer: *Lord I ask for Your blessing and favor as I turn toward You with all of my heart, soul, mind and strength. Help me to know You in spirit and in truth.*

139

"For I shall proclaim the name of Yahweh. Oh, tell the greatness of our God! 4.He is the Rock, his work is perfect, for all his ways are equitable. A trustworthy God who does no wrong, he is the Honest, the Upright One!"
Deuteronomy 32:3-4 (NJB)

Do you proclaim the Name of the Lord? Do you tell of the greatness of our God? Is He the Rock beneath your feet? Do you stand upon Him and His promises? Another word for "perfect," is "complete." He will complete his work in your life! Does that encourage you today?

All of these qualities of God are the opposite of what you experienced in your relationship. And if you had an abusive father as well, it may be hard for you to see God the Father as he really is.

Where the men in your life have not supported you or had your back, God is your Rock.

Where the men in your life did little for you, God is working perfectly for you.

Where the men in your life pursue the opposite of justice, your God is working justice for you.

Where the men in your life could not be trusted,

She is Free Indeed

God is ultimately trustworthy.

Where the men in your life did you wrong, God does no wrong.

Where the men in your life lied to you, God is the honest One.

Where the men in your life walked crooked paths, the Lord walks only in uprightness.

"God's way is perfect. All the Lord's promises prove true. He is a shield for all who look to him for protection." Psalm 18:30 (NLT)

Reflection: Think of specific ways that the Lord the opposite of your former partner.

Prayer: *Thank You, Lord, that You are the opposite of all of the things abusive men in my life have demonstrated to me. Clear my vision so that I can see clearly who You are.*

❊ 140 ❊

"Of Benjamin he said, 'May the beloved of the Lord dwell in security by Him, who shields him all the day, And he dwells between His shoulders.'"
Deuteronomy 33:12 (NASB)

Deuteronomy 33 contains the blessing that Moses pronounced over each of the tribes of Israel before he died. Today most Jews are no longer able to trace the tribe from which their family originated. However, the New Testament teaches that non-Jewish Christians have been adopted into Israel and we therefore can access all of the blessings of Israel.

The blessing given to the tribe of Benjamin is one of the shortest, but also the most intimate and beautiful. Do you know that you are the beloved of the Lord? Do you know that He shields you all day long? The word for shield in Hebrew is, *chaphaph*, which means to enclose, surround and cover. The image of dwelling between His shoulders is so beautiful and profound. In Hebrew, the word for dwell is *shakan*, which means to settle down or to abide. Are you able to allow the Lord to settle you? It means that the Lord holds you right up to His chest, He keeps you safe in His arms the way a loving parent comforts a child.

Ask the Lord to show you a picture of this today. Ask Him to help you to physically feel His presence wrapped around you today.

She is Free Indeed

"The eternal God is your refuge, and underneath are the everlasting arms."
Deuteronomy 33:27a (NIV)

Reflection: Picture yourself held in the Lord's arms with your head on His chest. Does that bring you comfort? If this feels threatening to you, how else could you imagine the Lord bringing you comfort today?

Prayer: *Lord, Thank You for adopting me into Your Kingdom. I ask for the blessing of the tribe of Benjamin today. Help me to trust Your covering over me. Help me to stay safely in Your arms.*

❋ 141 ❋

"As long as you live, no one will be able to resist you; I shall be with you as I was with Moses; I shall not fail you or desert you. 'Be strong and stand firm, for you are the man to give this people possession of the land which I swore to their ancestors that I would give them." Joshua 1:5-6 (NJB)

In Joshua 1, the Lord addresses Joshua whom He has chosen to take Moses' place in leading the children of Israel into the Promised Land now that Moses had died. The words, "be strong and stand firm," are repeated 3 times in this chapter. Joshua is one of only two people of the adults who had left Egypt whom God had allowed to live to see the Promised Land. Joshua saw everything, the plagues on Egypt, the Red Sea being parted, water coming from rocks and food falling from the sky. He had witnessed battles where the tiny army of Israel had wiped out other nations. Of all people, you would think that Joshua would not need a reminder of the power of God. Yet God instructs this mighty, faithful servant *three* times not to be afraid!

The Lord knows we are weak. He is patient with our failings. He doesn't lean down from Heaven and smack us upside the head every time we doubt. As He was patient with Joshua, so He is patient with us. So today, stand firm, take courage. The Lord who has been with you in past is with you right now and will be with you always. He is not going to fail you. He is not going to desert you. He is going to fulfill His promises to you!

"Finally, be strong in the Lord and in his mighty power."
Ephesians 6:10 (NIV)

Reflection: Ask the Lord for the assurance you need from Him today.

Prayer: *Lord give me Your strength and courage today. Help me to remember Your faithfulness.*

142

"Now, give this order to the priests carrying the ark of the covenant, "When you have reached the brink of the waters of the Jordan, you must halt in the Jordan itself." ...As soon as the priests carrying the ark of Yahweh, Lord of the whole earth, have set the soles of their feet in the waters of the Jordan, the waters of the Jordan will be cut off; the upper waters flowing down will stop as a single mass.'" Joshua 3:8, 13 (NJB)

This is an interesting passage on faith. When the Israelites were escaping Egypt, the Lord parted the Red Sea in front of them. He brought water out of a rock for them and rained manna from the sky for them. In each of these situations, God simply acted. But now, at the final stage of the journey, the Lord gave the command for the Israelites to act *before* the Lord did the miracle. He instructed the priests to carry the Ark of the Covenant (which symbolized the Lord's presence) into the river. They had to get their feet wet. They had to trust that the Lord was going to make a way for them through the Jordan river, which at this time was in flood season. The crossing was most likely around 100 feet wide and the river at that time was probably more than 10 feet deep. The current would have been intense.

Sometimes the Lord calls us to take the first step in faith. The sight of the Jordan river at that time would have been daunting. But the Lord sent the Ark of the Covenant first before the Israelites. God might call you to take steps in faith that make no sense. He

She is Free Indeed

may ask you to get your feet wet in trusting Him. But know that even though you cannot see it, His presence goes before you. Trust in His unending faithfulness.

"And when those who carried the ark came into the Jordan, and the feet of the priests carrying the ark were dipped in the edge of the water (for the Jordan overflows all its banks all the days of harvest), the waters which were flowing down from above stood and rose up in one heap, a great dis-tan ce away at Adam, the city that is beside Zarethan; and those which were flowing down toward the sea of the Arabah, the Salt Sea, were completely cut off." Joshua 3:15-16a (NASB)

Reflection: Think of a time in the past where the Lord met you when you took that first step. How did He carry you through that situation?

Prayer: *Lord, give me the faith to take the first step when You call me. Thank You that You always go before me.*

❊ 143 ❊

"Joshua said to the two men who had reconnoitred the country, 'Go into the prostitute's house, and bring the woman out with all who belong to her, as you swore to her that you would.' The young men who had been spies went and brought Rahab out, with her father and mother and brothers and all who belonged to her. They brought out all her clansmen too and put them in a place of safety outside the camp of Israel." Joshua 6:22-23 (NJB)

When Joshua sent spies into Jericho, a prostitute named Rahab welcomed them into her home, hid them and then lied to the authorities to keep them safe. In return the Israelite spies told her that she and her loved ones would be saved when Israel invaded. They did ultimately save her and her family, and they became a part of Israel.

Not only did Rahab become a part of Israel, she ended up marrying Salmon who was of the tribe of Judah, and she became the mother of Boaz who eventually married Ruth, the Moabitess. She is in the direct line of Jesus' descendants. Rahab is one of only 5 women mentioned in the lineage of Christ. It is amazing and telling of how God sees and uses all people, regardless of circumstance. We now know that through God's grace and ability to see into her heart that Rahab moved from the despised position of a prostitute into a woman redeemed through love, and welcomed into one Israel's prominent families.

She is Free Indeed

This story is beautiful because it shows the grace and mercy of God. He took a broken, fallen woman, raised her up, gave her a family and a remarkable heritage. God can and does use anyone. There is no one he has ever rejected or only allowed to serve Him on a limited level. None of your past mistakes count anymore. Christ is in you; He beautifies you with his righteousness. There is nothing you cannot accomplish if the Lord leads you in it.

"This means that anyone who belongs to Christ has become a new person. The old life is gone; a new life has begun!" 2 Corinthians 5:17 (NLT)

Reflection: Is there something in your life that is hanging over your head making you believe that you are somehow not fit for the Lord's work? Let the Lord speak the truth of his complete redemption over you today.

Prayer: *Thank You, Lord, that my past has no effect on my future with You. Thank You for your cleansing, healing and forgiveness. I offer myself to You today; use me for Your glory.*

144

"And Joshua said, 'Alas, Lord Yahweh, why did you bother to bring this na-ti on across the Jordan, if it was only to put us at the mercy of the Amorites and destroy us? If only we could have settled down on the other sidthof Jordan! Forgive me, Lord, but what can I say, now that Israel has turned tail on the enemy? The Canaanites, all the inhabitants of the land, will hear of it; they will unite against us to wipe our name from the earth. And what will you do about your great Name then?'" Joshua 7:7-9 (NJB)

These verses follow the story of the defeat of the Israelites by the nation of Ai. The reason for the defeat was that one of the Israelite soldiers had stolen and hid some property that the Lord had said had to be destroyed.

Joshua uses some harsh words with the Lord here. The first sentence is fairly sarcastic. The second sentence is hostile. In the last verse Joshua is accusatory and even mocking, "And what will you do about your great Name then?" The Lord answered Joshua by telling him why the defeat occurred and gave him instructions for finding the culprit and punishing him. But the Lord does not call Joshua to account for his words.

In the Psalms as well, there are many examples of people speaking freely and openly to God, holding nothing back. These are often referred to as the lamenting Psalms.

She is Free Indeed

While the Lord in no way encourages harsh words, He seems to tolerate them with the understanding that humans need to vent sometimes. All emotions and the ability to feel emotions are a gift from God. Processing them and working through them with Him is a healthy expression of healing.

*"Why is life given to a man
whose way is hidden,
whom God has hedged in?
For sighing has become my daily food;
my groans pour out like water.
What I feared has come upon me;
what I dreaded has happened to me.
I have no peace, no quietness;
I have no rest, but only turmoil." Job 3:23-26 (NIV)*

Reflection: What do you need to get off your chest today? Tell the Lord about it, and don't hold back!

Prayer: *Thank You, Lord, that You are a safe place I can go to when I need to vent. Thank You for loving me no matter what. When I cry out to You in anger and frustration, I ask that You meet me there and help me to sense the depth of Your love for me.*

145

"But among the Israelites there were still seven tribes left who had not re-ceived their heritage. Joshua then said to the Israelites, 'How much more time are you going to waste before you go and take possession of the country which Yahweh, God of your ancestors, has given to you?" Joshua 18:2-3 (NJB)

After the Lord had led them by miracle after miracle to the Promised Land, the Israelites still had to fight to claim the land the Lord had promised to them. At this time, Joshua was getting older and he knew he would be dying soon. While much of Israel had already settled in their lands, Joshua got upset with the 7 tribes of Israel that had not yet claimed their territory. Their inheritance was not given to them on a silver platter. They were going to have to fight for it. But the Lord had promised that He would be with them and that He would ensure their victory.

What is your Promised Land? What dreams has the Lord put in your heart? What special skills has He gifted you with? What are your passions? It is time to stand up and fight for them. It is not going to be easy. The enemy will fight you every step of the way. But as you keep taking steps forward, the Lord is with you, fighting alongside you.

Ask the Lord what steps you can take today to enter into the fullness of your inheritance. And remember you do not ever fight a battle alone.

She is Free Indeed

"So now we must cling tightly to the hope that lives within us, knowing that God always keeps his promises!" Hebrews 10:23 (TPT)

Reflection: Do you have faith that God is going to do what He has promised to do? If not, why?

Prayer: *Thank You Lord, for the place You have brought me to. Show me today what I need to do to lay claim to Your promises to me.*

❈ 146 ❈

"On the contrary, you must be loyal to Yahweh your God as you have been till now. Yahweh has dispossessed great and powerful nations before you, and no one so far has been able to resist you. One man of you was able to rout a thousand of them, since Yahweh your God was himself fighting for you, as he had promised you. Be very careful, as you value your life, to love Yahweh your God." Joshua 23:8-11 (NJB)

These verses are in Joshua's final address to the nation of Israel before his death. The Hebrew word for "loyal," here is, *dabaq*, which means to cling, to cleave and to keep close. You cannot passively serve the Lord. You must consciously, actively, cling to Him every day. He must be your source, your all. He must be the reason that you live. People who do not know Jesus try to find life's meaning in family, in sex, in entertainment, money, fame, and power. All of these things are temporary, none of them are lasting or infallible. None of them satisfy beyond the moment.

The Lord is not passive in His love for you either. He brought you out of that destructive relationship. He parted the Red Sea for you to escape. He continues to fight battles for you every day. The words, "be very careful," in Hebrew are translated, *shamar*, which means to keep, watch and preserve and *meod* which means muchness, force and abundance. And "to love" here is also the word *dabaq*. These verses are cautioning us to keep extremely diligent watch over ourselves to ensure that we are always keeping close to the Lord.

"Let not steadfast love and faithfulness forsake you; bind them around your neck; write them on the tablet of your heart. So, you will find favor and good success in the sight of God and man." Proverbs 3:3-4 (ESV)

Reflection: What are you clinging to for help today?

Prayer: *Lord, help me to hold fast to You. Help me to never be distracted by other things as I seek to have my needs met. I choose to trust only in You.*

147

"And the Angel of Yahweh appeared to him and said, 'Yahweh is with you, valiant warrior!' At this, Yahweh turned to him and said, 'Go in this strength of yours, and you will rescue Israel from the power of Midian. Am I not sending you myself?' Gideon replied, 'Forgive me, my lord, but how can I deliver Israel? My clan is the weakest in Manasseh and I am the least important of my father's family' Yahweh replied, 'I shall be with you and you will crush Midian as though it were one man.' Gideon said, 'If I have found favour in your sight, give me a sign that you are speaking to me.'" Judges 6:12,14-16 (NJB)

God chose Gideon to be His instrument in delivering the Israelites from the oppression of the Midianites. Gideon was not exactly excited about this. He was about the least qualified person the Lord could have chosen. He was very doubtful and quite obviously did not want to take on this role. Even though an angel of the Lord appeared to him, he was still mistrustful. God granted him the sign and then twice more Gideon asked for signs and the Lord provided them. God did not express frustration with Gideon and neither did He give up on Gideon. God gave him what he needed to fulfill the mission God had for him. After God gave Gideon those signs, as he led the people into battle, the Lord greatly reduced his fighting force. He pared down the army of 32,000 to only 300. Imagine how Gideon must have felt knowing he was facing an entire army with just a handful of men.

She is Free Indeed

How about you? Do you struggle with faith, especially when it seems like you don't have enough of whatever it is that you need? Most of us do. And yet the Lord is faithful and does not condemn or get upset with us. He simply provides. Your weaknesses don't matter when God wants to use you. There was no way the army of 300 could possibly wipe out the Midianites. It had to be the Lord. So, give the little you have to the Lord today and watch Him work wonders through you.

"But God chose those whom the world considers foolish to shame those who think they are wise, and God chose the puny and powerless to shame the high and mighty." 1 Corinthians 1:27 (TPT)

Reflection: What perceived weaknesses hold you back from serving the Lord today?

Prayer: *Lord I bring You both my strengths and weaknesses today. I trust that You can use me no matter what. Help me to trust You every step of the way.*

148

"Now it happened, that same night, that Yahweh said to him, 'Get up and go down to the camp. I am putting it into your power. If, however, you are nervous about going down, go down to the camp with your servant Purah; listen to what they are saying, and that will encourage you to go down to the camp.' So, with his servant Purah, he went down to the edge of the outposts of the camp." Judges 7:9-11 (NJB)

In the verses above, God, in His infinite patience, sees that Gideon, His servant, is still worried. Gideon did not express his worry to the Lord this time, but the Lord recognized it in him and gave Gideon yet another sign. When Gideon and his servant went to spy on the Midianites, they overheard someone talking about a dream he had had and he named Gideon as a fierce warrior. The Lord wanted Gideon to know that He was with him and would be with him every step of the way.

Having been in an abusive relationship, you most likely have some significant fear triggers. You probably struggle with anxiety. Gideon struggled with anxiety himself. But with the Lord with him, and only 300 men, he managed to route the Midianites. He went on to be a powerful military leader and the Israelites even wanted him to be their ruler. (He chose not to be). As long as he lived, the Midianites remained in subjection to Israel.

She is Free Indeed

Our limitations do not stop what the Lord can do through us. With Him beside us we can accomplish incredible things. Do not let fear hold you back. Know that if the Lord calls you to something, He will give you what you need to do it.

"For it is God who works in you, both to will and to work for his good pleasure." Philippians 2:13 (ESV)

Reflection: Think of something that triggers your anxiety today. How can you give that over to the Lord?

Prayer: *Thank You, Lord, that You are bigger than my fears. Thank You that You come to my aid when I feel weak and anxious and that You do not condemn me for it. Help me to trust You when I am afraid.*

❊ 149 ❊

"So then the Lord, the God of Israel, dispossessed the Amorites from before his people Israel; and are you to take possession of them? 24 Will you not possess what Chemosh your god gives you to possess? And all that the Lord our God has dispossessed before us, we will possess."
Judges 11:23-24 (ESV)

This passage is taken from the story of Jephthah, the son of an Israelite man and a prostitute. In this time period, the Ammonites made war with Israel. The Israelites knew Jephthah to be a fierce warrior and came to him to lead their army. He went on to defeat the Ammonites. The words above are from a message Jephthah sent to the king of the Ammonites. He reminds them that the Lord had given them great victories in the past. The Lord had taken Israel out of captivity. By saying, "are you to take possession of them?" Jephthah is saying that no one, great or small, can take anyone away from the Lord. The NIV reads, "what right have you to take it over?" The CEV reads, "Now do you think you're going to take over that same territory?" As you move through your journey of healing, it is important to claim each small victory as a step forward. It will be tempting at times to fall back into old habits, patterns and behaviours. It may even seem easier to go back into the old relationship or fall into a new relationship that is equally unhealthy. As you go through your journey, ask the Lord to reveal to you each victory. Ask Him to help you claim it and continue to move forward.

She is Free Indeed

"For I am convinced that neither death nor life, neither angels nor demons, neither the present nor the future, nor any powers, 39 neither height nor depth, nor anything else in all creation, will be able to separate us from the love of God that is in Christ Jesus our Lord." Romans 8:38-39 (NIV)

Reflection: What has been taken away from you in your own life? What has the Lord put in your heart that can never be taken from you?

Prayer: *Thank You, Lord for all of the victories You have given to me. Thank You that nothing can separate me from Your love, and no one can take me out of Your hands.*

❊ 150 ❊

*"He raises the poor from the dust
and lifts the needy from the ash heap;
he seats them with princes
and has them inherit a throne of honor.
"For the foundations of the earth are the Lord's;   on
them he has set the world." 1 Samuel 2:8 (NIV)*

These words are found in the prayer of thanksgiving Hannah made to the Lord after she had finally conceived a child. Hannah was desperate to bear a child. She cried out to the Lord and He heard her and granted her request. Hannah's story of calling out to the Lord in desperation can be an allegory for the desperation of living in the pain and suffering of abuse. The words, "Ash heap," can also be translated as dunghill or refuse heap. Is there any place lower than living in a garbage dump? And is there any place higher than a glorious throne? God loves to do the impossible, the improbable and sometimes, even the absurd. Putting a beggar on a gilded throne? That sounds crazy. But God loves to find people in miserable circumstances and turn their lives around. He did it for you. His are the foundations of the world.

What part of you is in the dust today, in mourning? What part of you feels like garbage? What are your needs? Do you trust the Lord in all of them? Do you believe He wants to deliver you? Bring your poverty before the Lord, ask Him to heal and bless you.

She is Free Indeed

Ask Him to show you what that throne of glory and honor looks like for you.

"I know that the Lord secures justice for the poor and upholds the cause of the needy." Psalm 140:12 (NIV)

Reflection: Do you believe the Lord will meet all of your needs? Do you trust His timing?

Prayer: *Lord I bring my needs before You today. I ask that You fill me up and be glorified through me.*

Contact Rachel

Instagram: rachelcoxbooks
Facebook: Rachel Cox-Author
RACHELCOXBOOKS@GMAIL.COM

www.ingramcontent.com/pod-product-compliance
Lightning Source LLC
Chambersburg PA
CBHW071953070526
44583CB00015B/1180